TALES OF OLD MUTARE

by
Old Mutare Authors

MAPLE
PUBLISHERS

Tales of Old Mutare

Author: Chris Mvere

ISBN 978-1-83538-393-3 (Paperback)

Published by:

Maple Publishers
Fairbourne Drive, Atterbury,
Milton Keynes,
MK10 9RG, UK
www.maplepublishers.com

A CIP catalogue record for this title is available from the British Library.

Tales of Old Mutare: vol 1

ACKNOWLEDGEMENTS

Thank you to all our parents who made it possible for us to grow up at Old Mutare Mission. Thank you to all the Old Mutare youth who inspired this work with their nostalgic stories about life at Old Mutare shared in Mission Boys and Girls "whatsapp" group formed by Tariro Darikwa and Ndingaitei Mvere. We also appreciate the distinguished contributions to this book made by Dr Ralph Nhiwatiwa, Professor Chido Johnson, Rudo Dzenga , Hammerskjold Chidawanyika , Vimbai Darikwa. Farai Nyamajiwa. Shupikai Noisi. Rudo Chifamba .Tapiwa Sithole and Tino Chimbadzwa among others in terms of technical and inspirational guidance. Thank you to the Old Mutare Missioners Book Team for the dedicated effort to put this body of work together and to all the Authors who took their precious time out to recount their memories and put them to paper. We acknowledge the United Methodist Church which built this wonderful place and maintains it to this day.

We Thank God for the energy we have every day to go out and do incredible things by His Holy Spirit in the name of Jesus Christ.

Tales of Old Mutare: vol 1

The Authors

The Authors of this book have one thing in common: They all grew up at Old Mutare Mission or spent a significant amount of their youth there. With the majority having been born there they share a sense of belonging to its history and this work is an effort to add to that history of Old Mutare Mission, home of Hartzell Schools and Africa University.

1. Ndingaitei C Mvere
2. Tariro Oswald Darikwa
3. Dr Ralph Nhiwatiwa
4. Tapuwa Nzara
5. Jonah Dozva
6. Farai O Mvere
7. Namatai A Mukono
8. Shupikai Noisi
9. Vimbai F D Darikwa
10. Farai Nyamajiwa
11. Rudo Chifamba (nee Kanjanda)
12. Tapiwa Sithole
13. Ndozvi Kamangira

The Old Mutare Missioners Book Team

This book has been produced through the dedicated work of this team comprised of members who have spent time living at Old Mutare Mission and understand its Ethos.

1. Ndingaitei C Mvere - Chief Coordinator
2. Rudo (nee Kanjanda) Chifamba - Financial Coordinator
3. Proffessor Chido Johnson - Artistic Coordinator
4. Farai Nyamajiwa - Marketing Team
5. Vimbai Darikwa - Marketing Team
6. Tapiwa Sithole -Editor
7. Tino Chimbadzwa - Illustrator
8. Tariro Oswald Darikwa - Administrator
9. Dr Ralph Nhiwatiwa
10. Shupikai Noisi
11. Dag Hammerskerjold Chidawanyika
12. Rudo (nee Bingepinge) Dzenga

FOREWORD

This book is a culmination of collaborative efforts by individuals who are currently spread across several countries and continents but remain joined together by their inception roots to their place of birth and childhood, Old Mutare Mission in eastern Zimbabwe. They are like tender seedlings planted in one nursery and as they mature and grow little shoots, the gardener uproots and disperses them all over the wild forest where they get lost but with time, they all mature into massive trees which outgrow the rest until they begin to spot each other from far locations and start linking up again.

The authors are from all walks of life, representing a wide spectrum of professionals, age groups and lifestyles which gives the book a unique variation of authorship styles. There is a clear focus on childhood memoirs of growing up in that special community. The tales reflect children's simple and naive perspective of community life, yet deep analysis of each story reveals important lessons for adults today.

Similarly, the obituary stories are written through children's eyes which see a lot that evades the adult eyes. Hilary and comedy are engraved in the stories. The accounts demonstrate the simple things which children take as heroism which they look up to in their years of growth.

I trust that these childhood reflections will provide the reader with a deep appreciation of the community life at Old Mutare mission.

Dr Ralph Nhiwatiwa

TALES OF OLD MUTARE

VOLUME 1

CONTENTS

INTRODUCTION:

Old Mutare Mission

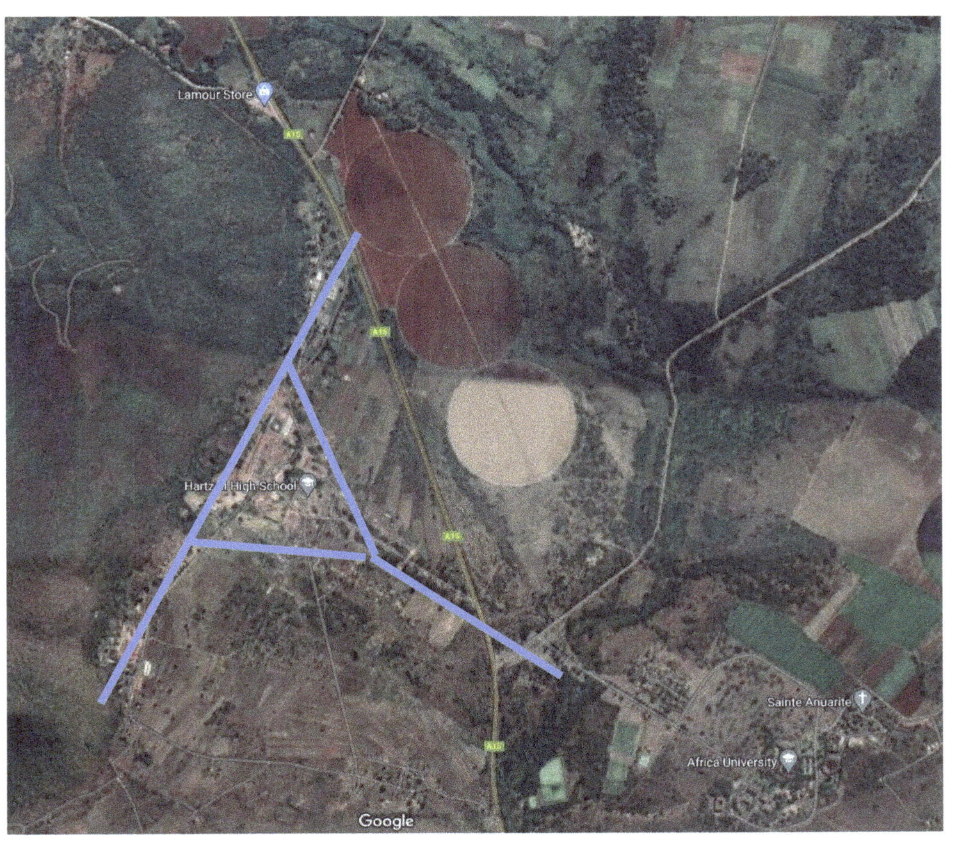

Old Mutare Mission

If you search for Old Mutare Mission on Google Maps today, and activate the satellite view, you will have to zoom in and out a lot until you find Mutare on the eastern border of Zimbabwe. Follow the road from Mutare through Christmas Pass until you find the road heading towards Nyanga. Just as you follow it, you will suddenly find a reddish area in between mountains and then you will notice the road heading towards the centre of the reddish opening. As you zoom in, you will see lots of buildings and when you zoom out again, behold you have an aerial view of Old Mutare Mission. A very historical place in the history of Zimbabwe, going right back to 1893 when Cecil John Rhodes put Mutare town there, before later selling it to Bishop Hartzell in 1897. It struck me when I looked at the Mission and the roads criss-crossing through it that it looks like a womb, and so it is.

I don't know if this was by design or coincidence, but what an allegory for what Old Mutare Mission is. The children and the students come to the mission as academic infants, and come out of Old Mutare mission educated and ready for tertiary education at higher institutions or for citizenry in Zimbabwe. However, the womb which nurtured them is often forgotten for its role in developing the student or person who comes out of

Old Mutare mission. You have the school and the church, which are central to building the student or person. But in order for the school and the church to function, you have the surrounding community of Old Mutare, who perform all the functions that a womb does. You have the teachers who educate the students, you have the maintenance staff that service the housing facilities at the mission for all the workers, you have the hospital that provides medical care. All these, work together to make Hartzell deliver the highest quality citizen for Zimbabwe. True to the womb allegory, all departments at the centre work in unison to nurture a person that then is delivered to the world.

This collection of stories is an attempt to screenshot the life in the womb, that is, Old Mutare Mission by those that were children of the staff members at this great institution.

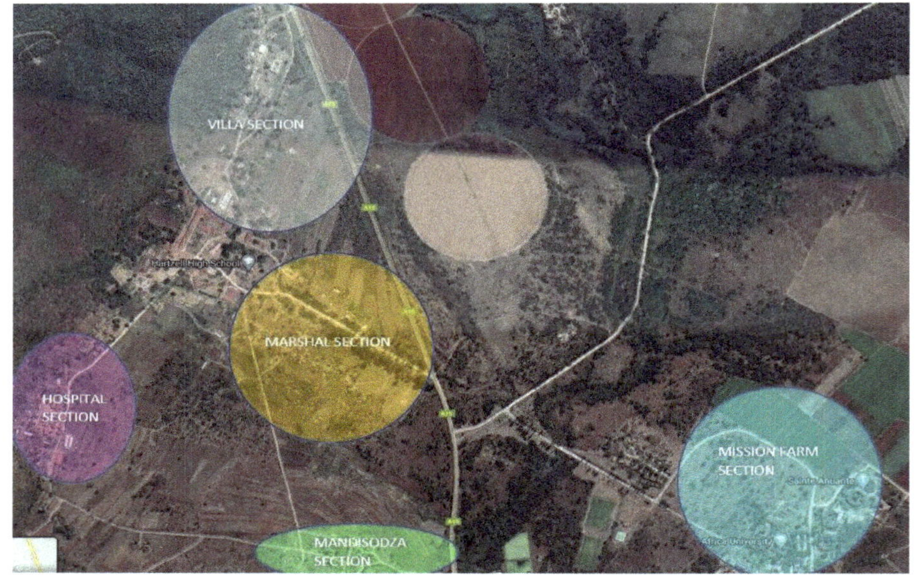

The Vision

It was said, and still reverberates in the collective psyche of those that hold Old Mutare Mission near and dear to their hearts, that once, Bishop Joseph Hartzell had a vision on top of Mount Chiremba, where thousands of voices were heard coming to this place for knowledge and leaving it to build Zimbabwe, Africa and impact the rest of the world. Visions and prophecies of God always come true. I remember in 1988, during one of our Sunday church services, when the then station Chairman Rev Dr Nhiwatiwa, announced to the jubilation of us all in the church that day, that Old Mutare Mission centre had been chosen to be the place for a new university by the United Methodist Church. Its name was to be Africa University.

It was as if God said it was not good for Hartzell to be alone in the garden of Old Mutare, and put Hartzell to sleep, took a rib from him and out came Africa University. Looking at each other magnificently, the church building at Old Mutare Mission is directly opposite to the chapel at Africa University, and the entrance roads to both centres are aligned to each other in beautiful geometry.

So, we envisage stories of and from this magnificent hub of learning to continue to be churned out to the end of publishing more volumes of like nature. It should never be undermined the role the womb plays in producing all the products of Old Mutare.

By Ndinga Mvere and Vimbai Darikwa

SECTION ONE (1): RUFARO NURSERY AND HARTZELL CENTRAL PRIMARY SCHOOL

Rufaro Nursery School

Chapter One (1)

According to the written records, it was on a morning on the 14th of June 1964 that parturition completed and I landed in a crib at old Umtali Mission Hospital. I was the fifth child and fourth son to John and Marjory Nhiwatiwa.

My arrival in this world coincided with a unique time in the history of the United Methodist Church in Rhodesia. The bishop, Ralph Edward Dodge had earned political notoriety for opposing the white minority rule led by Mr.

Ian Smith, and was sadly deported by the government. I can only guess that the bishop was really popular among the indigenous Africans, for which reason I undeservedly ended up with Ralph for my name. However, the strong influence of my vernacular Shona Language made it difficult for most folks to articulate 'Ralph' leading ultimately to a coarse version of 'Raru' which has stuck to this day.

Number 32 Marshal Road was our home, a gloomy looking piece of edifice lacking in architectural style, with tiny windows, asbestos roof and pale-yellow walls. The front flower garden was an impressive collection of beautiful poinsettias and hibiscus shrubs. The backyard was a polar contrast with a thriving poultry industry, numerous chicken houses, heaps of chicken manure, and heaps of grass. This was my father's passion.

I grew up among my siblings and countless cousins. In infancy, as soon as l could figure out that the smiling face behind the breast l was suckling was my mother, and that the one without breast milk but with sharp bristles of beard which irritated my soft brow, was my father, a decision was made to send me off to nursery school.

Looking back, this was rather precocious. I had barely evolved from crawling and was still struggling with the art of putting one foot in front of the other when my name was registered for first year at the local nursery school. The little I knew about nursery school came from watching my older brother, going to school all scrubbed up and neat and to return completely soiled up, muddied with fresh bruises for each day. I could imagine a pack of kids perpetually fighting and tumbling. Even the alphabets and number figures in his school book seemed to be fighting and tumbling.

Chapter Two (2)

The First Step

My first ever excursion out of my cozy enclave of 32 Marshal Road came on a wet morning in January 1967. Joy and exhilaration filled the house as I was scrubbed, dried and 'vaselined" head to toe before donning my best shirt and shorts. At this tender age, l had not fully grasped the essential skills of continence and was then faced with the humiliating prospects of carrying around cloth diapers which were tucked in a paper bag. My brother Aggrey was delighted to accept the honorable task of supervisor and overseer over me, but adamantly refused to carry the paper bag.

The trip to Rufaro nursery school involved tracking on a muddy path cutting through the mission to the foothill of Chiremba Mountain. A whole band of excited toddlers from the neighborhood joined us. With our little sandaled feet, we rushed off, hopping over puddles of rain water as we raced through muddy paths.

My first close up encounter with a 'zongororo' (millipede) was awesome. The black double legged creature was cautiously snaking its way across the path when it came to a halt. A small touch with a stick to its head was all it needed to give up and roll up in utter frustration. I could not take my gaze off the shelled snails. I loved the way the slimy creatures were gracefully sliding in the mud, never in a hurry but quick to withdraw into their shells at the first sign of trouble. The tall grass on the path side was like a forest to my diminutive stature. The black ants scurrying up and down the anthills were monstrous to me. Even the crickets and the locusts looked huge as if they could carry me away on their huge claws. I gripped Aggrey's hand harder.

Our route took us past the mission's maintenance department where the most amazing piece of American engineering was on display; the Massey Ferguson tractor. We stood in awe. Uncontrollable childhood curiosity overwhelmed me as I gazed at it for long. With a huge jostle, Aggrey hauled me back on road to Rufaro. Having walked past the headmaster's house and the tranquil parsonage, we entered the church yard. The church building itself was huge and I thought its sharp pinnacle was even more striking. The grounds were leafy with a clear air of serenity.

With determination we reached the great Beit Hall which was to our left and the tuck-shop on the opposite side. Some colorful pine trees occupied the space in between. The brick walls of the little tuck-shop were covered by colorful marketing posters of all sorts of goods, from sunlight soap, to mazoe orange crush drink. The red and white Coca-Cola board was irresistibly enticing, even to the most juvenile eyes. Thankfully Aggrey tugged me along and kept me on course to our final destination. The last stretch of the road was up-hill and rocky; however, we made it.

Chapter Three (3)

The First Day

The loud squealing, wailing and screaming heralded our arrival at Rufaro Nursery School. On the hill-side was this gigantic colonial style building with intimidating large doors and windows. The front garden was teeming with toddlers and kids dashing around, tumbling and falling in uncontrollable jubilation. Suddenly, a deafening clanging sound came from a huge metal bell hanging from the Msasa tree in the middle of the playground. Silence immediately prevailed as all the kids ceased their reckless activities and fell into a single file and walked into the school room in military style orderliness; we followed.

The classroom, was a large space with plastered floors and bright white ceiling roof. On the floor were numerous wooden boxes of various colors; red, black, green and white. Each kid excitedly leaped and perched on the boxes like little owlets and proceeded to ogle at me and my paper bag curiously. A few boxes were unoccupied and we quietly chose to sit on the front ones.

Quite unexpectedly, there was a rapturous outburst of "good morning teacher Angie", with all the kids springing to their feet. I am sure l was forgiven for mistaking the figure standing at the doorway for a giraffe. Teacher Angie was the tallest earthling l had ever set my eyes on. She cautiously avoided knocking the doorway top with her head and made her way to the big table in front. Her fingers were equally long and bony. I immediately resolved to avoid ever being knuckled on the head as Aggrey had warned me. She had a focused penetrating gaze, but when she eventually smiled her whole face transfigured into amazing beauty. While the rest of us carried around the cheap fragrance of lifebuoy soap, teacher Angie had a peculiar sweet smell and the Ambi-special make up gave her a final angelic finish.

Once a gain a spontaneous rapturous salutation rocked the room; 'good morning teacher Linda'. Almost consuming the whole doorway was a chubby pleasant being with little arms sticking out like fins. She proceeded to paddle her way to the front of the classroom and greeted us with a shrieking little voice. A brilliant smile dissected her face making little dimples on her cheeks. She spoke slowly and each word seemed to take a lot of breath out of her. I am sure she wished she were taller or at least shared her anthropometry with teacher Angie. Her style of attire was voluminous and occlusive but amazingly colourful. The daily class routine was simple. Teacher Angie would pull out a thick book and read out the children's names, while the appropriate respondents went 'present' and sticking up the right hand. It seemed the order was alphabetic as she took a while before she read 'Ralph Nhiwatiwa'; by which time l had mastered the 'present!'

My classmates were a peculiar bunch, but a generic appearance of ring worms over the heads seemed to unify us. I do not know which missionary had convinced our mothers of the panacea potential of gentian-violet, some devilish looking purple concoction which was smeared on our heads and lips for any sort of ailment or any other anatomical region requiring medical attention. The net effect was a collection of little heads with purple patches like circus muppets.

Chapter Four (4)

Creamed Buns

My little mind was exhausted and slowly slipping into my usual mid-morning nap, when the powerful aroma of fresh cream buns flooded the room. We all lit up like electric bulbs as we watched the local baker place on the table a tray of shiny buns with gaping slits filled with white cream. The pleasure and joy of this special delicacy, together with a mug of warm milk was unparalleled and the memories remain etched in my mind to this day.

Following the bun and milk time, we were all required to take a nap for half an hour on reed mats (rupasa) on the classroom floor. I recall these moments of peace as this was the only time to listen to the beautiful orchestra of birds' sounds from the rich birds' life in Chiremba Mountain. Doves cooing, eagle shrieking, wood peckers knocking, the gruff guttural calls of the hornbills and so many others.

The rest of the morning was spent in loud sing-a-long rhymes, hymns and in games. 'Tumawoko tumawoko, tunoita zvakanaka, tauya kuona Mary and twinkle twinkle little star', thrilled us. I soon fell in love with the life at Rufaro Nursery School.

In the far, right corner, next to the kitchen, was a large box containing a massive collection of real treasure; toys. There were plastic dolls, tops, jungles, little cars and buses, you name it all. Each morning, soon after the bun and milk time, Linda, with assistance from the bigger boys, would carry the treasure box to the outside garden, and with a ceremonial 'hurray' tip it over to spill the treasure on the lawn. A mad scramble would ensure. For the boys, the most popular was a little choo-choo locomotive, while the girls trampled each other for dolls. Scuffles and punching's were a daily thing. Toy time took a good part of the morning before the switching to games and singing. We loved "hwai, hwai uyayi kumba, mhumhi dzakapera kuenda kwaMutare". We would make formations of groups and tease the approaching 'wolves'. On reaching a critical point of provocation the wolves would charge and their prey who would scream and dash in all directions.

"Paushamwari wedu tega, tega zvedu," was a little rhyme by friends who would hold shoulders, bragging and boasting about their special friendship, often provoking envious hit back by other school mates. "Zai rakaora, zai", this was my best, where we would sit in a big circle and the first runner holding a 'rotten egg' would encircle speedily and on picking his target, he would drop it on the fellow's back before dashing for his life with victim in hot pursuit. Failure to be caught would assure him of an empty sitting slot and would be cheered as a winner. The process repeated many times. The bigger girls loved "nyuchi kana yaruma pamupambwe, tomato so-so-sososo, elizage, age, agegegege!'

Chapter Five (5)

Toilet Training

As I mentioned earlier my entry in nursery school was premature and happened before l had mastered the art of continence. Nevertheless, I quickly learned from my fellows that by mumbling something like 'may-ya-goja-toyet', in the teacher's ear she would point in the direction of the toilet and grant you passage to the little toilet at the back of the classroom. My full diapers were becoming a source of derision. The unpleasant stench would trigger waves of giggles much to Aggrey's dismay. To this end, I resolved to take control of my alimentary and urinary systems. I gathered the guts and went up to teacher Angie and whispered the magic phrase and to my surprise she pointed to the little toilet door, and for the first time in my life l was given passage to gentlemanly ablution. My little face beamed with a great sense of achievement as I made the inaugural toilet flash and emerged from the toilet bubbling with confidence to take my place on the box seat without a diaper.

As with most kids in the village, we were often bare footed but at some stage, fortune struck and my brother and I received a pair of '*Mutowenyembas*', which was a cheap type of shoe made out of cloth and rubber. *Mutowenyembas* were perceived very lowly in our circle of friends, for which reason we adamantly protested and chose to go to school bare footed. Our juvenile resolve was no match against authoritative parental instruction, so we found ourselves plodding to school in Mutowenyembas. Rather than facing the humiliating jeers at school, my brother hatched a plan to hide the demeaning footwear in the flower bush next to the entry gate of the school and retrieve them on our way back home. We did this each morning and the plan worked well for some time until one morning when Eddie, the school gardener, made the shocking discovery. With beaming eyes and a gaping mouth, Eddie proudly presented his discovery before teacher Angie right before the whole class. Identifying the culprits was not difficult. We were soon paraded and ordered to wear the *Mutowenyemba* shoes while those long hard knuckles played marimba on our brow and purple heads.

Chapter Six (6)

The Great Escape

While my memory maybe waning on many events of nursery school life, there is one little story which I recall with absolute clarity. We were still using the big building up the Villa hill when I suddenly came up with an idea to run away from school forever. Pure juvenile naivety drove me to plan my flight and escape. So, on the day in question while everyone was in the middle of the popular song "shiri yakangwara uri kuendepi, uya,

uya titambe", I sneaked behind teacher Linda unnoticed and with a burst of energy, I dashed off and headed downhill on the muddy path, amid the wild jeers from my classmates. Teacher Linda was in hot pursuit. Suddenly, I was airborne and landed on the soft bosom of my pursuer. My desperate kicking and screaming were futile as she easily carted her fugitive back uphill. I recall that in my tantrum I tore off a beautiful bow from her favorite light green dress.

Chapter Seven (7)

Our Mothers

Rufaro Nursey School was run by Methodist women's organization called 'Ruwadzano Rwemadzimai', RRW for short. Although they received generous charity support from fellow Methodists in the USA, a good part of the funding was supported by the local women's activities, such as, selling hand-knitted goods and jumble sales. All families would take turns to provide some extra snacks for the school kids. The commonest donation was a special type of fried cookie which we called 'fat cookie' which was very filling. (Seriously, I won't recommend these to the reader).

Many other teachers joined over the years. I recall Mrs Mudzengerere and Mrs Mutimbanyoka. The mission pastor in charge often paid visits to the school. The teaching program and curriculum was designed to improve children's behavior and encourage early learning in preparation for primary school. Christian and Bible teaching formed the core curriculum. We were privileged to have learnt of the popular Bible stories such as David and Goliath, Joseph in Egypt, Jonah and the fish, Noah and the Ark and so many others. I am absolutely convinced that those old educators planted vital seeds of faith in our young souls and deserve credit from all of us.

Organized school trips were a thriller. The one special trip was by bus to a local shopping complex which was located on the other side of Chiremba Mountain. The official name was L'armor Cash Store but somehow everyone called it 'paFricks'. The Chinaka bus was often used for this trip. The old shop owner took pride in handing out the bottled cold drinks from an old refrigerator. Common brands were Coca cola, Fanta, Canada Dry and Cream soda.

At Rufaro Nursery school we were privileged to welcome many visitors from the USA. We admired them so much for their pleasant nature, friendliness and extreme generosity. Their English language sounded funny and often incomprehensible to us. One such visitor was a young enthusiastic teacher by the name of Teddy DeWolf. He owned a big camera and took numerous pictures of our class. On instruction we yelled 'cheers!' at which point he would pull the hanging code to produce a frightful flash.

Over the years 1967 to 1970, the location of the school was shifted twice, first to the pink house across the road next to the dam, and later to the old Chimbadzwa hall which remains the current location. Over this period, our class matured from thumb sucking infants to bright pre-school boys and girls.

Chapter Eight (8)

Valediction And the End of Year Function

The annual Christmas party and end of year function were the climax of joy at Rufaro Nursery School. Customarily, this was held in the month of December on a Sunday afternoon at the huge Beit Hall next to the tuck-shop. My valedictory function was in December 1970. The run-up to the great day was marked by endless rehearsals in dramas, plays and songs. The event was a great attraction to parents and members of the community, who would occupy the rows of benches in the main hall, while we proudly took the spotlight on the elevated front stage. The gigantic maroon theatre curtains closed us off in the backstage, while the teachers organized us into neat rows. Traditionally, a strong former student would be assigned the task of winding open and closing the huge curtains, a task which they undertook with such pride.

On instruction from teacher Angie, the huge curtains would be opened, allowing the flood of lights from the main hall to brighten the stage, exposing the excited faces of the cast, amid loud cheers and whistling from the audience. "Joy, joy, my heart is full of joy" and "mauya, mauya vabereki" (welcome parents), were our usual opening songs. The planned choreography often failed into disorderly jumping, twisting and rabbit- like hopping. The nativity play of the birth our Lord Jesus Christ was the main attraction. I do not clearly recall what role I played, perhaps one of the shepherds who fell flat when the angels appeared.

A formal graduation process for the senior students who were crossing the gulf from Rufaro to the Kraal school (grade 1) would follow. In a single file, clothed in little black gowns and four corned caps, we would be presented with our nursery school certificates, while the crowd erupted in great applause and clamor.

From Mitchell's bakery in Umtali, we were always privileged to receive the Zambezi cake. This was a special vast confectionary coated with thick cream. Like a surgeon, teacher Angie would cautiously cut it up into numerous little blocks and we each picked one. I still dream of the great sugary taste which together with mazoe (an orange drink) is part of the eternal nostalgic memoirs for the boys and girls who grew up at that special place called Old Umtali Mission.

To the boys and girls who grew up at Old Umtali Mission, this little nursery was special. This little institute was inception for greater future achievements by thousands of present-day professionals who are spread throughout the whole world. For these great educators, lawyers, engineers, ministers, senior government officials, doctors, university academics and church ministers, the foundation of their success lies in this humble little institute, Rufaro Nursery School.

~THE END~

By Dr Ralph Nhiwatiwa

The First Day at Kraal

Attending primary school in the early 1980s at Old Mutare Mission was really an adventurous ordeal blended with meeting new people of diverse backgrounds, since the primary school accommodated everyone including children from surrounding farms (Franklin, Meikle, Guy, Coke Norris, Berry). It was the only primary school in a radius of approximately 7 to 8 km. I remember, my first day at Hartzell Central Primary School (HCPS), at the kindergarten, popularly known as "kuKraal". We were all lined up in the open space in front of the classrooms, the prospective grade one students for 1981. We were then asked to walk up to the teachers for the entry interview, which was touching your left ear with your right hand passing through the center of your head.

If you managed to touch the ear then you would have passed the entrance interview and got admitted, but if you failed to touch your ear, you would be then told to come back the following year. (It was a tough entrance interview for kids with small bodies and a big head! I wonder how some people I know got through this one!). So, after passing the entrance test, the grade one teachers would be lined up in front, sharing the students, one per teacher at a time as they passed the entry interview, like the way we share playing cards in a game of "Crazy Eight". So, through this way we were all allocated our classes with our respective teachers.

The real drama began after the class allocation, and we were now all being taken to our respective classes. When some friends/cousins noticed that they had been separated into different classes, they started crying, asking for their mothers, and refusing to move to the classroom if the other friend was not there. Once inside the classrooms, more drama emerged about scrambling for chairs and which tables (group) to sit on, while others were sneaking out to look for classrooms where their friend(s) had been allocated to. (Some permanently changed allocated classrooms this way!).

During that first day, I was placed in Mrs Nyakuengama's class. At breaktime we were told to go outside and play, so I went outside and met up with my friend Farai Chidzungu, who was in a different class. Farai and I stayed relatively close to each other, down at the end of Marshall 2 near the football pitch, popularly known as "Kuground rebhora". So, since everyone was now outside their classrooms, Farai and I assumed that classes had ended so we made our way home, playing all sorts of games along the way. When we got to my home, one of my aunties asked us why we were back from school early, then we told her school had finished and narrated what happened. She laughed and then told us we had left school at break time, that was when it only dawned on us that there was a period called breaktime at school, just to refresh and go back to class. Later during that first week, there was an announcement in all the grade one classes that the first bell to ring signified the start of what was known as breaktime, and we weren't supposed to go home, so we were expected to come back into class when the bell rang again. The teacher would then later announce when it was the bell to go home. So, I suppose Farai and I were not the only ones who left school at breaktime during that first week.

By Tapuwa W L Nzara

Breaktime Snacks

At Hartzell Central Primary School (H.C.P.S), break time was one of the best times for most of us. It gave us a breather from the learning ordeals with the teachers, giving us a chance to open our packed snack boxes or go to the tuck-shop to buy nibbles, while some other enterprising kids also sold snacks such as maputi, sweets, nuts, etc. to generate a bit of pocket change.

One of my best memories of a break time snack, was having four of us, contributing 5 cents each, then going to the tuck-shop to buy a fresh half loaf (half bread) which we savagely tore apart among ourselves like wild dogs without any proper sharing etiquette. I remember one time, a novice joined our break time snack savage group then was asked to go and buy the half bread after the contributions had been made, while we waited patiently outside the tuck-shop. When the novice returned with the half bread, he then presented it to the group thinking that there were some sharing protocols, and then within seconds, he remained just holding the khakhi paper that the half bread was wrapped in! So now he had to chase around the group members begging for a piece of the bread and eventually every member of the group tore a small piece for him.

One of the most sought out break time snacks, were nuts popularly known as "manuts". Years later after high school, I only got to find out that the nut's official English name is Pecans (*Carya illinoinensis*). The pecan is a species of hickory, native to northern Mexico and the southern United States in the region of the Mississippi River. The tree is cultivated for its seed in the southern United States, primarily in Georgia, New Mexico, Texas and also in Mexico, which produces nearly half of the world total. These nuts were brought and sold by children from the surrounding farms, I think specifically from Berry (Bheri) and Meikle (Mikiri).

So, nuts were a delicacy which had a lucrative business, but the challenge was how to acquire the nuts by these school kids. They had to go and steal them from the farm orchard fields which were guarded by guards and half the time when they got caught, they would endure a thorough beating. The nuts were usually sold in 2 kg plastic packages of sugar, and two or three nuts would cost like 1 cent back in those days in the early 1980s. Since nuts were a highly sought-after delicacy, there were even mafia like gangs during break time, who would move around with razor blades to slice open the plastic packages where the nuts were sold from, and then they would all fall to the ground, resulting in other kids rushing to pick up the free manna.

Children who lived within the mission, would usually come to school with packed break time snacks of bread, sandwiches or boiled eggs which then introduced the break time snack exchange; 1 boiled egg could get you half packet of the 2 kg nuts depending on your negotiation skills, a slice of bread or a sandwich would get 10 nuts. For children from the farms, most of them did not have easy access to eggs or bread at home, so this break time snacks barter trade became quite popular especially among friends. I remember, always sneaking out with extra boiled eggs from home for facilitating the break time snack exchange with my guys.

Years later, I walked into OK supermarket, and I was shocked by the price being charged 'manuts' per kg that I saw, the snack we practically had almost free of charge at primary school.

By Tapuwa W L Nzara

Jonah Akatumwa NaShe

My name is Jonah Kumbirai Dozva. I was born at Old Mutare Mission Hospital in December of 1973. I went to our local nursery school - Rufaro Nursery School, where my teacher was Miss Mazaiwana. In 1979, I expected to graduate from the nursery school to grade 1. I am convinced to this day that I was not allowed to graduate and proceed to grade 1 because I was too short. I was short and very dark.

This disappointed me, but I made a brilliant plan that I was going to go to grade 1 anyway. So, when schools opened in 1980, I dressed in my best blue scotched suit, and turned up to Mai Nyakuengama's class. I must have looked very tiny because she immediately ordered me to go back to nursery school. I cried and rolled on the floor in protest and drew the attention of Mai Rugayo, who then took me to her classroom, sat me on a chair by her desk and asked me to write my name on a piece of paper. I successfully wrote my name, and she was happy to admit me into her class, since I had proved to be better than many other kids who were crying in terror at being in school. I was so excited to be finally in grade 1 with my friends.

During the start of the second term of school, our headmaster, Mr Nyanhanda, summoned my parents to his office and asked them why they had not bought me a school uniform and why they had not paid my school fees. "But he is still in creche, Mr Nyanhanda!" replied my parents. They were shocked to be told that I had already completed the 1st term as a pupil and that school fees was now due. This was because I never told them that I had followed my friends to grade 1. So, every morning I would dress in my creche clothes especially the blue scotch suit and go to grade 1 instead. My parents had to buy me khaki uniform and thus my school life began.

My adventures in school did not end there. After school on my way home, I would walk past the woodwork shop. There was a fruit tree there, where Matohwe, also known as “Azanza” or “Goron Tula” fruit grew. One day I decided to have some of the said fruit. I started throwing stones at the fruits in the hope that some would fall to the ground. One of the fruits fell on the seat of a nearby parked tractor, ready for a “hill start”. I hopped on to the tractor and in the process, I found myself in the driver’s seat. I decided to find out what would happen if I released the hand brake. The tractor started rolling towards the school ground as I controlled its steering. Soon I could not control it as it picked pace and I went into a panic mode. I heard Mr Ndadzungira shout, “Iwe Jonah dzikapo!” (Jonah jump off). In a panic I jumped off the speeding tractor and ran away leaving the tractor to hit an anthill close to the Ndemera house.

Grade 2

I did my Grade 2 in Mr Makoni’s class at Kraal school. Once a week, every Wednesday, the whole primary school would gather in the Ehnes Memorial Church; those from C.P.S, B.I and Kraal. One of the Wednesday devotions at church, Mr P.K Mudiwa asked Tapfuma Karumbidza to sing a song. Tapfuma and I were enemies stemming from an earlier altercation over *Matohwe* fruits. Of all the songs he could sing he chose to sing the song "*Jonah Akatumwa NaShe*" based on the story of the Biblical Prophet Jonah. I was the only Jonah at Hartzell Primary School and I thought he was singing about me. I started crying and I ran away, home bound, from the assembly. Mr Makoni, my teacher, came to our house to bring me back to school. I told him to his laughter that I thought Tapfuma was singing about me.

Grade 3

On another occasion, my teacher, Mr Jumburu, beat me up and I got so upset I ended up breaking windowpanes behind the BI. Mr Nhamo Chimuswe saw me and charged at me, so I ran away through the gum trees until I got to the orange orchard near the Dzobos. The debacle earned me some serious spanking from my dad. That was the last time my father spanked me.

By Jonah Dozva

SECTION TWO: PRE-TEEN AFTER SCHOOL ADVENTURES

Bhurumango Business (1984)

I grew up at Old Mutare Mission during a time that was very exciting for us young kids who knew nothing about the recently ended war of liberation. All our parents had the grand hope of a new Zimbabwe. My father was a renowned 'A' level Maths teacher at our local school, Hartzell High and we lived in the Villa section of Old Mutare. There were other sections or suburbs too in the mission, such as Marshall, Mandisodza, Hospital, and

Mission Farm. There was a good number of kids in all sections of the mission. Our parents were employees of the Mission or school. Villa Section had some of the biggest houses in the mission which were occupied mainly by teaching staff of Hartzell High School.

My story happened in 1984, and during that time my best friends were Reginald Chidawanyika and Andrew Mhere. However, in this episode Regi was not involved. I wonder where he was. However, the three of us were very good friends in the same grade four class. Andrew and I were like *Chivhindikiti na Ndonda* because Andrew was quite chubby, and I was skinny. After school we would get home, change our clothes, have our lunch, usually sadza and muriwo or nyama, then disappear into the mission for the day's adventures, only to return home just before night-time.

So, one afternoon, Andrew and I were walking on the main road through Villa section from the tuckshop where we had gone to buy our favourite afternoon snack of peanuts, which we called "*hwambo*". They came in a little plastic pack and cost a fortune of 5 cents, sold at the musika by the ladies such as Mai Dozva, under the bottlebrush trees in front of the tuckshop, or at the B.I under the big cyprus tree by Mai Sithole. So, *hwambo* was very popular those days. Whenever we had some pocket money, one of the things we had to do was to quickly go and buy "hwambo". Just what we lived for those days.

However, on this day walking past the Nyamajiwa yard we saw our younger friend Gwinyai Nyamajiwa enjoying a juicy *Bhuru Mango* from one of their many such trees in their yard. Of course, in mission courtesy, he happily invited us to have our choice of the delicacy from their tree. We gladly enjoyed the *Bhuru Mangoes* as we called them, huge yellow juicy divine fruits, would certainly take you to heavenly bliss with your first bite. Lovely. I remember how we enjoyed that afternoon while chatting about Knight Rider and the A-team, arguing about whether a car could ever fly like Kitt, or it was just fiction. I usually made sure to convince everyone that it was real.

The chatting and eating of the mangoes continued until Gwinyai's father asked him to feed their dog, "Danger". Off course Andrew and I not wanting to leave our debate nor the delicious Mangoes, we decided to stay on. Our discussion now progressed to whether we thought Kitt was better than the Dukes of Hazard car. In the midst of this we were soon interrupted by the voices of "maSecondary" or the boarding girls going up to their Villa hostels. "Can we have your mangoes please?" they asked. We believed the trees in Gwinyai's yard had hundreds of mangoes, so we offered the boarding school girls the mangoes, and they went on their way very happy.

The next day whilst walking along the tuck shop road, we found ourselves in the tree enjoying its offerings, but this time Gwinyai was nowhere near. We enjoyed the mangoes again, however, more of maSecondary shouted to us from the road asking for the mangoes. "Can we have some please?". We told them we could not give them any mangoes, after all, we were not even the owners. As if they knew how our boyish minds worked, the girls offered to pay us for the mangoes. Andrew and I looked at each other and remembered our first love, *hwambo,* and gladly received our first 2 cents from these 2 girls and we thought we needed 5cents for *hwambo*, so we upped the price and started selling the mangoes. We could not believe our luck and started making even more money. At the end of the shift, we had enough to buy a pack of *hwambo* each. Business was exciting. The next day we were back and making more money. Business was so good we started taking the green raw mangoes to a ripening store at the big unoccupied white house. Wow, how wonderful this was!

Just as we were about to start selling the ripened mangoes, we happened to visit our tree on a Saturday morning, in time for the "Masecondary" coming from the morning study session, and we waited patiently for our customers. However, on this day Gwinyai was around, playing in their yard near the mango tree. We invited him to "our tree". We wondered how it had not occurred to him to make some *hwambo* money from their mangoes. “What do you mean?” he asked. We explained to him how the masecondary loved the mangoes so much that they gave us money for them, and we innocently shared that we were making a decent profit from the mangoes. “You are selling our mangoes!” Gwinyai exclaimed. We tried to respond creatively, "Well not exactly Gwinyai, the girls donate the money to us after we give them the mangoes.” "Ndaa komumangarira kuna Daddy. *(I am going to report you to my dad)*”

Oh, not the D word. That got us startled in our pants and we hurried from the tree into the fields south of their yard. We knew we were in trouble now and had little time to process anything after he invoked the D word. During our days, “Daddy” meant strict discipline if you went out of line, especially with the use of a green peach tree branch or if in the case of a serious crime, the sjambok was applied. Our violation here seemed to us to be in the sjambok level, and we ran into the fields away from anyone, and no one could find us for a good 3 hours until they gave up looking for us. Andrew tired from running, being *Chivhindikiti,* exclaimed that, “I will never do this again”. I remember saying “*Ko mango dzese dziya kuwhite house toita sei nadzo?”,* ie “what would we do with all our mangoes at the white house?". "That would not be nice to leave all those mangoes rotting", I said. "Let's sell them first, then we hang up our business". I am sure like always, I got Andrew to agree with me.

After 3 hours of just being by ourselves, hiding from the search party that was looking for us, Andrew decided to throw in the towel and went back home. I think he was hungry. I stayed in the bush by myself for a while. Eventually I decided to go home and face the music. I met Andrew wiping tears from his eyes and I could see white stripe markings in his legs. Yes, he had gone through trial and sentence in an instant. Oh, I knew I could not run forever and proceeded home fully aware what awaited me. My dad came back from *kwaFriks* merrily as usual, and the night would have passed uneventfully had it not been for my CIO siblings that gave a report to him on what I had done. To my surprise, my dad was amused by the story until he heard that I had been running around in fields all afternoon. Unfortunately, I was not so lucky, I met a familiar foe called Sjambok. That was the end of our *Bhuru Mango* Business: *Chivhindikiti na Ndonda* Pvt Ltd.

By Ndinga Mvere

Inferno

Back in the day, Paul Gumbere and I were wanderers and scavengers looking for treasures wherever we could find them. One fine day I came from school, removed my uniform, and jumped into my wanderer's gear, which was of course a lousy t-shirt and some pants. As I was walking out the door of the kitchen, I noticed a single matchstick lying lonely on a cupboard. I decided to relieve it of its loneliness, picked it up and put it in my pocket and thought nothing else of it. I looked for my available fellow wanderers and, on that day, Mataza was not available, but Paul was. I passed by his house and off into the woods we went.

We made a beeline past the Jiwas (Nyamajiwas') house, into the fields that were behind their house. As we walked Paul picked up an empty match box. Immediately I exclaimed, "what a coincidence, you picked an empty match box and look! I have a matchstick in my pocket". This happened by the tree where the Nyamajiwa twins (Farai and Tafadzwa) and I used to practice some Karate moves, or so we thought. We did this by climbing up the tree and then free fell on our butts hoping our butts would be as tough as nails. It is by God's grace that our spinal cords are not broken or shattered after being subjected to this unmitigated act of boyish lunacy. I digress.

I suggested that we light up a fire and see what happens. Paul's response was unequivocally negative. I insisted but Paul was adamant. My negotiation skills were summoned into overdrive and my diabolical plan prevailed, but not for long. What then ensued left me with an egg in the face. Paul was right until adventure blinkered us both into a lull. I lit the match. Right there, the lure of adventure sucked us in. We watched the fire grow from a tiny flicker into a colossus, but this again was not before a heated debate about when to extinguish the flames. I had suggested that we put out the fire when it was ankle high, but Paul thought it was too early. Roles had reversed. When the fire was knee high, I again suggested it was time to put out the fire, but Paul was enjoying the drama and could not shrug off the lure of the incredible.

When flames were up to our waist, we then immediately both agreed that it was time to put out the flames. As soon as we tried to stomp the flames with our feet, the flames spread as though possessed. The fire literally took a life of its own. We broke some flimsy green branches from trees near-by to put out the flames, but it was an exercise in futility, the flames only grew worse. Each attempt to quench the flames resulted in exponential rise in ferocity. The fire had now morphed from a little flicker into an inferno. The flames got so angry that Paul and I had to flee for our lives. At that moment the flames had won. Watching from a safe distance, we were petrified as the conflagration started to claim the whole southern district of the fields and taking the whole territory at a jaw-dropping speed. Meanwhile Paul and I were safe and sound looking at the raging inferno with other onlookers who were wondering what idiots had started the fire. One onlooker, Sisi Getty, the DeWolfs' maid, suggested that someone should call the police, so they got to the bottom of this. The suggestion shot fear right through our impressionable hearts provoking instant confessions, accusations, and counter accusations. Another 'inferno' of words between Paul and I had just started.

The inferno turned its sights on Rev E.K Nhiwatiwa's house and all his belongings, causing him to rush out of his house screaming and yelling at anything that could hear. He used to live where the Mheres (George, Andrew, Callista, Veronica) used to live; but for those newer to the mission where the Reavises, or the Ngirandes lived. The good Reverend learned that I was one of the culprits and his ire was now targeted at me since I was older than Paul and consequently should have known and acted better. It did not help that some years later he would become my History teacher at ZJC. He remembered, and yes, to this day when he meets my brothers, he inquires about the one who started the fire, not the student he taught for 2 years. As the inferno approached his fowl run, he rushed to open it and screamed in a language the chickens could understand as they also saw the fire coming; they must have heard, "run, save yourselves!" The chickens came out and fled. His poor vegetables could not run as the chickens did so they gazed unto the heavens and helplessly awaited their demise as judgment day had arrived. The whole community came together, some with branches, some with hoses, and some with buckets of water to fight the raging fire. The battle was fierce but the fire was defeated causing it to turn southward towards the Chieza house and the fields in the south; the community then flanked the enemy and fought valiantly. There was neither loss of life nor property damaged. Well, as for the police, we leave that to your fertile imagination.

By Farai Mvere

You Wanna Be Starting Something Breakdance (1984)

The early 80s was a very interesting period for us growing up at old Mutare. This was because some of the best entertainment was being churned out from the United States and we were accessing it through our local Zimbabwe Television (ZTV) and Zimbabwe radio (ZBC). This was the big era for Michael Jackson, Tina Turner, Lionel Ritchie in music, but it was also the time of the A Team, Knight Rider, TJ Hooker, Blue Thunder and World Federation Wrestling (WWF).

One phenomenon that began this time was the Breakdance craze that got to Old Mutare. I particularly welcomed it and dived right into it. My Uncle, Sekuru Blessing Charowedza and his friend, Tafara Mutimbanyoka introduced me to this fun way of dancing. My nephew, Cliff Rundu, was also a big fan he already had moves of his own, I was in good company. I was soon introduced to the brothers, Nhamo and Kudzai Mumbiro, who had recently come to Old Mutare from USA. I used to watch them practicing moves and soon I began to learn how to breakdance.

We used to perform at weddings, even though I remember only being involved at one of the weddings and dancing in the Beit Hall. Most wedding celebrations concluded in the Beit Hall where rehearsed dancing brides' maids and groomsmen would entertain the wedding guests, which usually was the whole mission. On such occasions, the Breakdancing group would perform, and I soon earned a reputation among my peers of being good at breakdancing.

I remember being asked by my grade 4 teacher Mrs. Mawoyo to show the class how to breakdance, and I demonstrated how to moonwalk, crawl like a worm, head spin, and robot motion. I got a standing ovation and cheering from the class, and my father was amused by my interest in breakdancing to music from Michael Jackson; a passion I still possess to this day.

By Ndinga Mvere

Mt Chiremba Secret Mission

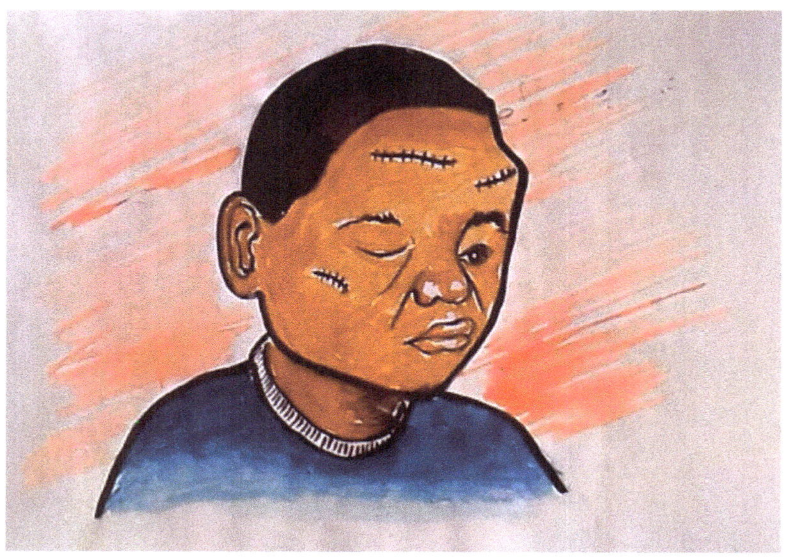

Growing up at Old Mutare Mission was full of adventure and fun. There was something extra special about the place, it was spiritual too. I personally experienced all three. I am grateful to the Lord Almighty, who protected my friends and I as we took adventures that were very risky. As kids, we were oblivious of the dangers. We placed ourselves in things such as encounters with snakes and old pits left by the first British settlers.

One day, I met Simba and Tino close to the swimming pool. The two boys were on a mission to climb Mt Chiremba, and their next statement was, "Do not tell anyone please." I wanted to join this mission right away, but someone equally crazy for adventures was missing. This special someone was Farai (Fari). On enquiring whether he was joining, the answer was, "He is coming or he is already in front of us." This was now game on. My only concern was, why Fari had not planned this with me as always. We then walked towards the Biblical Institute (B.I) enroute to conquer Mt Chiremba and enjoy the view that Bishop Hartzell had experienced. This was also where he had the vision of the Hartzell learning institutions, both primary and secondary, with Africa University as the icing.

My two young companions were all speeding ahead as I was busy looking for my friend both behind and ahead of us. I had a fresh headache as the eldest in this secret adventure. If by any chance things went south, I would be held accountable and answerable. I needed some back-up. Fari was nowhere to be seen. As we progressed towards the main ridge that joins the hospital mountain and Mt Chiremba, it became clear that my best friend was neither in front nor behind. Tino and Simba were all good because they had each other. As it became clear that it was going to be just the three of us, I then decided to stop looking for Fari. I was now the eldest, and I knew

I would be roasted for leading two young lads on a mountain adventure if we were caught or an incident happened. We were only allowed to climb with an approved responsible adult.

The trip to the top was quick and easy. The only bottle of water we had was empty, but the joy and euphoria quenched our thirst. We had conquered Mt Chiremba without being spotted, and as heroes, we stood looking over Old Mutare Mission and MRID. I then said, "Now team, we have to go down before it's dark or before we raise suspicion of our whereabouts." I knew Fari would never have told any soul down below of this secret mission which we equated to an undercover CIA mission.

I chose to lead the way down because it dawned on me that we had less than an hour before 4pm (if you know you know). The Karanga people say, "*Mandikurumidze akazvara Mandinonoke*". As we reached the steepest part of the decent by the fire guard, I made a fatal mistake. Mission boys and girls know that you need to sit down and control the descent with the heels of your feet. I believed I could pass any tough military training including the Air Force of Zimbabwe. The steep gradient and force of gravity forced me down to the extent that I started running down without any control. I tried to bear-hug a tree that was on the edge. This was my next mistake, I missed it and I had the most terrifying fall of my life. Up to now I have never experienced a near death situation like that. I remember being upside down like I was on a diving board then landing on the back. At this point I passed out.

The next moment I heard Tino and Simba saying, "Can you hear us?" I had rolled and somersaulted the whole length of that steep slope. A small bush broke my fall right on the L-sharp of the slope. I was lying on the back, my right leg caught on a V-shaped branch of a small tree. The two boys thought I was seriously injured and could not walk. I requested them to get my leg out of the branch. Adrenaline was probably full in my body, I got up and said, "Gents I am fine, let's continue." I looked at the point my fall was broken and realised any centimetre further would have seen the end of me. It was much steeper and full of rocks. Simba and Tino continued to talk of how terrifying the fall was, but it was no longer my concern. My whole body was like chocolate and clothes red from the soil. I was grateful that it was me and not the other two because of the matrix of age.

When we got to the B.I, the 1550hrs siren went and it was mission accomplished, but I had to get rid of the evidence, which was my chocolate covered body. We took the boys creed again not to talk. At this point I saw my bestie Fari, "Yeah, Namatai ko why *mandisiya*?" I said, "I thought you were in front or was coming". Fari then noticed how bruised I was but I did not have time to talk, I had to go home to take a shower and Fari came with me.

The missionaries built very good accommodation for their staff members. I avoided going into the main house and went to the cottage and took a shower, narrating to Fari what had happened. Fari was amazed by the soil the was coming off my hair and body; the soap form was turning red too. I then felt an irritation right on the top of my head, I had suffered a cut. I asked Fari to check it and yes, he confirmed it, but I was not going to the hospital or tell anyone. That night my mother noticed that I was not myself and I blamed it on the football exercise which was too hard, and I retired to sleep quickly before I was fully caught out. However, I knew she had picked it up and I tried to hide it. My father said boys, "Don't fight when you are out playing." Mother kept an eye on me, and she thought I had inherited a bold gene from her side.

The next day before morning devotion, Fari approached me to talk about my fall which he had been told could have broken my neck or back and I said, "Man that is water under the bridge don't raise it up otherwise *ndinopinda* busy." I even declined to have him check the crown of my head which had a cut.

The wound healed and I opened up about this incident many years later when I was in Form 3. Hair had temporarily stopped growing on an area about 1cm. I knew how to comb my hair, I told Kudzai my brother and mum after they were getting too curious about the bold patch. All my hair cuts were now at the barber shop, I knew how to avoid home barber "nechigero", all pocket money was saved for this trip to the barber.

I have never discussed this with Simba and Tino up to now, only Fari talks about the amount of soil I washed off myself. I thank God for my life on that day.

By Namatai Mukono

Nzviru and the Snake (1985)

As I have narrated before in my *Bhurumango* story, I had two best friends growing up, Reginald Chidawanyika and Andrew Mhere. In this episode I was with Regi, and am not sure where Andrew was; he could have moved to hospital section by that time.

One Friday afternoon after school, I went over to play with Regi. This was usually playing with wire cars, football, hunting birds with catapults etc. However, on this day my first stop was to be the berry fruit tree at the edge of their yard, next to the Musesengwas'. "Regi!", I shouted from their veranda, "let's go have *'Nzviru'*". These sepia brown coloured berries had just come into season and were quite tasty. The tree they were in was quite easy to climb, so we did occasionally spend time playing in it.

"*Ndinga shaa (Ndinga my friend)*, we can't go there today, a snake was spotted in the tree this morning", came Regi's unexpected response. "Really! What kind of snake?" I asked. "Snakes do not stay in one place. By now it's already gone. That was in the morning, it's afternoon now," I reasoned. I was not convinced that a sighting of a snake in the morning could warrant us postponing a visit to the *Nzviru* tree. All the times I had seen a snake, someone would be chasing it and it would run away fearing for its life, so I thought Regi was just being fearful, so I told him I was going alone.

I walked over to the tree and looked up, and sure enough there was no snake anywhere in sight, so I shouted to Regi saying he could come the snake had gone. I proceeded to climb the tree. This *Nzviru* tree was rather like a big shrub covering a large area. So, just as we always did, reaching for branches above and hoisting oneself up, I prepared myself to do so, but with no extra caution. I stretched to grab one of the branches above me, and just as I was about to grab it, an unusual sense of caution came over me. I stopped. I surveyed this branch with my gaze to the left to where it started, but I could not see any further as the branch disappeared within the thicket of others. I turned towards the right, and still it seemed to be going across just like other branches. I kept looking at this branch to my right. I peered below one of the thicker branches, and all I could see was a white triangular end to the branch I was following. It was at that moment when its reddish forked-tongue licked the wind twice. My God! Immediately, I was on the ground in dust, got up and shot towards Regi's house shouting, “Nyoka! Nyoka!”. Goodness me. I could not believe that I had almost grabbed that snake thinking it was a branch. It blended so well with all the other branches; my hand was over it before God’s grace stopped me from grabbing it.

Everyone around was startled and people came to where we were by the veranda. Whilst trying to rest on the veranda I soon noticed an unusual sensation on my arm around the wrist area. I pressed my hand onto the veranda floor and felt movement inside. Fracture it was. I timidly went home and was scared to tell my father that I had hurt myself, so I went and told my niece, Sis Catherine. I thought she would keep it to herself. Whilst

I sat in our bedroom, I saw my father through the window walk across from his study room. He had his unique step and since he was at pace, I knew I was in trouble. *"Waitwa sei",* translated, "What happened to you". I told him my arm was feeling weird but not painful. I expected a ticking off for climbing trees but instead he was gentle with me, rather asking to see my hand. I was then taken to the hospital and ended up with a white plaster on my left arm for 3 weeks. All for the love of *Nzviru.* Having the plaster was cool and it saved me from getting into trouble with Kuziwa Mawoyo. Later my best friend in high school. But that's a story for another day.

By Ndinga Mvere

The Hunting Games

As a team of boys living near a group of mountains, we had developed a habit of going up these mountains every Saturday. Together, we had a total of more than nine highly trained dogs. These dogs were even capable of bringing down a leopard. However, our main targets were usually the waterbucks, hares and even baboons (which we later fed to the dogs). On Sundays we joined the rest of the boys at the football grounds where the usual section versus section soccer matches took place. Normally, the Mandisodza village would win such matches. This was mainly because we had all types of boys; short stout for defence, long legged and fast for attacks, and the average ones who played the midfield. The village also had very energetic supporters, male and female, young and old. However, during one fateful weekend, our hunting style was to change.

It happened that one Saturday we were so lucky to catch three different animals, a buck, a rabbit and a warthog. Since we returned home late, we decided to do the sharing the following day, which would be on a Sunday. This was the same day our soccer team was supposed to play against the Villa team. Early on that Sunday, we began skinning, sharing, and obviously roasting some of the meat. This is when one of our female soccer supporters was stung by a big black wasp on her left cheek. Within a few minutes her head was terribly swollen, and her eyes closed. She was the lead vocalist for our supporters, and without her songs we were definitely going to lose. The atmosphere immediately changed. In a few minutes we transformed from the happy hunters to fierce warriors.

The group comprised of the experienced hunter, Farai, together with his younger brother, Munyaradzi, my brothers Tendai and Mazvita, Samuel and his brother Kenneth, Ndozviudzaani and his younger brother Rutendo, and Nangisai accompanied by his younger brother Kuziwa. Together we decided to hunt and kill all wasps within a two-kilometre radius of the village. Firstly, we moved from house to house making a thorough clean up. We then decided to go into the mountains since we believed that these mountains were the major suppliers of such insects. We used small branches from trees to destroy their nests, and I remember one of us who used his bare hands to clap on them. Our main targets were the *Munzambara* trees which are the main trees on which such wasps *(Marumamombe)* build their nests.

At first, we seemed to be victorious, and from the *Machiwenyika* mountain (which is the name of the mountain at Mandisodza village), we could see the Villa soccer team striker, Kudzai and his brother Cornelius, with the rest of their teammates, waiting for us at the football grounds. They were warming up in preparation for the coming game. Little did they know that we were caught up in some important business. The referee, who was also my grade seven teacher, was already blowing his whistle as a way of reminding our team that we were now needed at the football pitch. Spectators were already waiting to watch the likes of Zwaitwandiye and Victor displaying their skills. The likes of Luke and Shingirai would sometimes join in making the Mandisodza team even stronger than any other in the mission. Obviously, the team structure was a source of endless arguments when it came to money games.

Within a few hours, we had ravaged the whole mountain, killing a lot of these black wasps. Satisfied with our victory, we set back home with the whole team singing war songs. Our biggest mistake was that we used the same path we had used when going into the mountains. Obviously, we had not killed all the wasps, but merely irritated some of them. This was their chance to retaliate. It felt like we were being hit by live bullets. The victory songs turned to cries for help. *Pfumo renyuchi harina mununudzi*. Although these were not bees, the attacking format was just the same. No one could save us. The black wasp is a very dangerous insect. These wasps are aggressive and territorial. They use their long stinger to attack. Just like bees, wasps usually attack in packs which can be dangerous and deadly. People who are allergic to wasp stings can suffer from severe reaction that requires immediate medical attention. Unlike bees, wasps can sting repeatedly. People get attacked more by wasps because they tend to build their nests in homes and in hidden locations, as a result people are more likely to disturb their nests by accident. Ours was not an accident. We had asked for it. On this day the wasps were merciless. In trying to save ourselves, we ran through thorny bushes and rolled in stony grounds. We however managed to get to our homes where we got all sorts of treatment.

Meanwhile, at the football grounds, the referee had become restless. He was very much into soccer and could not understand how a whole soccer team could forget to fulfil its fixture. The spectators had to disperse. The youths who had cancelled their afternoon Scripture Union session were even more disappointed than the rest of the supporting crew. They could have made better use of their time. Anger was again ignited the following day, Monday, when my grade seven teacher, the referee, discovered that more than nine learners from Mandisodza were absent from school. It was maybe acceptable to forget about a soccer match but forgetting to attend school was a big NO. After some fruitless enquiries from Farai (the basketballer) and Shadreck (the reggae master), he decided to visit our village. When he arrived at Mandisodza he was already trembling with anger. This however quickly subsided when we presented ourselves before him. The majority of us could not even see him because our eyes were still closed due to the excessive swelling. He just drove back without saying a word. We knew the scores would be settled when we returned to school.

That was the last time we went into the forest. Some of us joined Ndinga's UMYF group, some Farai's basketball team, and those in the football team never missed a match again. Some female vocalists joined Cathy's reading club. I joined Tapuwa's bicycle team.

Dedicated to all those mission boys and girls who are no longer with us.

Surnames have been withheld to allow some of us to recall for ourselves.

May God continue to bless us all

By Shupikai Noisi

The Swimming Pool

One of the delights of our youth at Old Mutare Mission was being able to go and swim in the local swimming pool. It was a big swimming pool; about 5m wide and 20m long and probably going from a shallow end depth of 1m, to a deep end depth of probably 3m. The deep end was scarily deep, but I might be exaggerating because I am basing my estimation on how I remember it from back then. It was surrounded by a thick dark green hedge with two changing rooms; one for the boys and one for the girls, and a pool water treatment plant.

The swimming pool was a popular venue for all mission kids. We would often wait in long queues for it to be opened by either Dr Tepee, Ms. Strickland, or Mr Haas. These were the expatriate teachers at Hartzell High School who were responsible for overseeing the swimming pool. They doubled up as the lifeguards too. While waiting at the gate in the long queues, all eyes were in the direction of Ms. Strickland or Dr Tepee's apartments in anticipation that they were coming to open the gates to allow us to swim. On some of the occasions they would skip coming and we would walk back home thoroughly disappointed that the swimming pool had not been opened. Most of the time though, they would show up, and the moment we would spot them walking from their apartment with a drying towel over their shoulder, we knew it was time for fun. We waited in glee for the gate to be opened then we would rush to the changing rooms to take off our clothes and put on our swimming clothes and away into the pool we would jump.

While swimming was popular, we all had to have swimming lessons and be water safe first. I remember Mr Haas teaching us how to swim. We had to learn to swim across the width of the pool 10 times without resting before we could be allowed to swim at the deep end. It was an achievement to be allowed to swim at the deep end and I remember the excitement of going to the deep end and being allowed to use the diving board. Qualifying to use the swimming pool was a joy. It was a sight to see people basking in the sun around the pool, and by the time we left for home, many of us looked like ghosts because of the ashen skin colour ("shena") we had, and the red eyes from swimming with our eyes open in chlorinated water. I laugh at the image of this in my mind. Saturdays and Sundays were the most popular swimming days and I remember swimming from 1pm right up until just before 3pm when I would leap out of the pool, put my clothes on, and run home in time to catch the football commentary by Charles Mabika. If the soccer game was boring or Dynamos was getting beaten, I would run back to carry on with swimming. It was a lot of fun to us all mission kids; boys, girls and high school students. Lots of other naughty stuff used to go on in there of which Jonah Dozva was chief culprit, but that is a story for another day.

I nearly had a bad accident while attempting a back flip from the diving board. Only God saved me that day. I jumped up but did not push away towards the pool and narrowly missed hitting the diving board with my head as I went into the pool. I never attempted that again. I just remember surfacing from the water and seeing the teacher Mrs. Strickland or Mr. Haas come running towards where I was and people looking and asking if I was ok. Thankfully, I had missed it by a whisker. I thank God also that in all the time that we used to swim there we never had any mishap at that pool. There are so many things that we ought to thank God for during our youth.

However, 1992 brought our swimming experience at Old Mutare to an end. There was a nationwide drought that made water supply at Old Mutare an issue. The water at Old Mutare used to come in via a ditch from Lake Alexander and received at the tanks in the Villa area, where Mr Matongo used to run the water treatment plant. When the drought of 1992 struck, the water from Lake Alexander dried up and alternative water sources had to be sought. The water from Lake Alexander was so plentiful that all the residents of Old Mutare did not have to pay any water bills. We had both pure drinking water supply and ditch water supply for irrigating our gardens. As the drought ravaged the country, even the ditch water supply stopped.

Thanks to some international donations that were made, boreholes were introduced at Old Mutare and of course these were driven by electric power to draw the water and pump it to the water treatment plant to be distributed throughout the mission. This made water at Old Mutare an expensive commodity, and with that the swimming pool became an expendable luxury that was never used again to this very day. Along with the Economic Structural adjustment Program (ESAP) and many other things in Zimbabwe, 1992 may have been the end of the "independence honeymoon" of our young country. A lot of the simple pleasures we had like having a local swimming pool for young mission kids to play in, simply became unaffordable for our mission and not a priority. The drought ended but the source of our water at the mission was never retained. Hopefully one day someone will find value in restoring the swimming pool at Old Mutare Mission.

By Ndinga Mvere

Tariro's Adventures

My life journey started at Old Mutare Mission, born in the dirty streets of Marshal village. My dad was Mr Mcdonald Darikwa, and my mum, Mrs Annie-Grace Zimunya Darikwa. As kids, we spent most of our days in the Marshal valley and we slogged through the lush grass and rich red soil. My house is the same house where Jona Dozva grew up in Marshal section. I do not remember exactly when, but at some point, we moved. I must have been three when we moved to the big brown house next to the "baby house" at the hospital. Yep, that is what we called it. In the end, l had four siblings namely the late Chenai, the late Doris, Vimbai and Rumbidzai.

We grew up calling it *ku*Baby House (BH). During my early years my friends where from the BH area. The actual name of the place is Fairfield Orphanage. I remember l had a good friend called Nhamo. We went to nursery school and started grade one together, we were good buddies. My class teacher was Mrs Mwandiambira. One day l woke up to discover that Nhamo had found a new family, he had been adopted and I never saw him again. He vanished and up to now l have no clue where he moved to. I have never forgotten him. I wish somehow, we had kept in touch.

The mission residential areas had names, namely, Marshal 1, Marshal 2, Marshal 3, Villa section, Hospital, Mandisodza, MRID, Gum trees and Riverside. Our house was positioned at the bottom of the famous Chiremba mountain. We used to enjoy climbing the mountain on a regular basis. We enjoyed the view from Chiremba mountain. It was refreshing. Life was so good it would have been excruciatingly boring without challenges and thrills. We were forever fascinated by climbing to the summits as we used to learn something every time we got to climb the mountain. I will forever miss the thrill of the summit and enjoy the view of the mission. It was a different view as compared to the peak of Chiremba Mountain.

One summer afternoon, l went to collect mail from the hospital. As I stepped onto the stairs going into the main hospital, I saw the late Sekuru Mawoyo chatting with my mother. I remember the conversation vividly. Sekuru Mawoyo was pointing to where Africa University is now, saying in the future, they were going to build a massive university. I did not think l would live to witness it. Unfortunately, Sekuru Mawoyo has since been promoted to be with the Lord.

At Marshal we did not have a house phone, but when we moved to the hospital section, there was a landline in the house. Every time the phone rang, I used to scream and run very fast away from it, going to dive in my mum's arms. If I was walking past the phone and it happened to ring, I would run whichever side my mum was. When I had grown up, I was told about the story, and I would always laugh about it and try to dismiss it.

The school was less than a mile from the hospital. During our early years, we would be escorted to school by the health care assistants who used to look after the orphans. On rainy days, mixed with luck on our side, the ambulance driver would take us to school and drop some at Rufaro Nursery School. After school, someone would come and escort us back home. School started from 8am to 12 noon. After school, we would walk home as a group. On our way, we would walk past the high school orchards. If we happened to meet Mr Nhiwatiwa, he would allow us to go and harvest oranges and nectarines. This really made us happy, and he became our favourite teacher. We would continue going home munching the fruits. The only problem was that we were little, so we were only able to hold two to three oranges in our hands. We did not have back packs, but a few lucky ones had bookcases. They would load oranges in them, which gave birth to another problem; the bookcases would be too heavy to carry. Often, the nursing aids would come to their rescue and carry them. The orchard was being maintained in a very immaculate condition and students, *ndiwo waive ne duty rekucheka hedge idzodzo.* Unfortunately, years down lane the orchard caught fire and the Cyprus hedge surrounding it was destroyed. This was the end of the orchards.

I remember very well during our last years in primary school, right into high school, going to the study hour at night. We would go in the orchards and quench our thirst and enjoy ourselves before proceeding. We were never in trouble although this was not allowed.

After school

During our years in primary school, the period after learning was ironically the best part of being in school. It was a time packed with action and drama. We would look forward to school simply because of the fun that came after the formal schooling. The fun was even amplified during weekends and school holidays. We used to be very naughty, always trying something new, so going back home after school was full of adventure. In most cases we would start by executing missions we had failed to complete the previous day. We had all the fun, and we never spent time watching tv, we made our own story lines outside. We had too many exciting adventures to explore, some were very dangerous, but fortunately nobody died.

In the hospital gardens were a lot of fruits. We used to enjoy eating bananas (stealing) but the gang had a few people in it. The gang leader was mainly Chenjerai Chambara, with the other gang members being, Gerald Zimunya, Tariro Darikwa, Daniel Madanhi, Vimbai Darikwa, to name a few. As one walked past the primary school garden, heading towards the hospital, there was a dirty pathway heading towards Chiremba mountain, *vaibva vapinda mumabanana* orchards. *Asi tisati tapinda muma*banana, we would split ourselves; some would be tasked to go and do surveillance spot checks, making sure *vanamukoma* Rivers Chapotoka and crew had left for lunch.

On the way, we would snape some sticks in a certain way to make sharp blades. *Ndiwo aiwe mabhemba edu eku ndodonhesa mubanana.* Once we got the 'all clear' message, we would go and select *ninga yemabanana yaiwe* ready *kundopfimbika.* This operation was executed silently using sign language. As four or five lads, *taitenderedza mubabana* with our sticks *totanga kubaya baya muti uya kusvika vadonha.* The rest of the crew would be watching *kuti muti uri kudonhera kupi.* Munhu 1 *ndiye aizosheedzera kana s*ign language *yaramba kushanda muti vawekundonda.* This was done *kuti tisapondwe nemuti vawekudonha.*

Muti wadonha, taibayabaya chimai cheninga to separate it from the *mai* stem. *Tapedza, tainohwandisa zininga riye raiwe rakakura, apa isusu tichiri vadiki-diki* in body size. *Kuusimudza* was another mission *asi taiusimudza* with no trace *kuti vaendepi.* At this time *isusu tinenge tavana* spot *yekundo pfimbika zininga redu. Tapedza kudaro taibva tananga kuswimming ku*hospital dam. At times *taiti tave kufukunura marara taibva tasangana neimwe ninga yaibva or yakahwandiswawo ipapo* presumably by the garden workers. *Taibva tatsvaka imwe* spot *topfimbika, todzoka tondoba ninga iye topfimbika* elsewhere.

After about 5 days we would come back for a feast. *Chainakidza ndechekuti munhu vose* would be present *ninga yaibva isina kubiwa taitonongora mabanana* and would share equally. We would take turns *kunhonga, taizoiti ini nonge, uyu nonge kusvika yapera. Aizowandisa* for little people, but *taiwe nemazano ekumatakura kuenda kumba asi aisasvika kumba chaiko. Taimahwandisa* somewhere *munhu wese aripo. At times taizodzoka kunotarisa kuti aibva here.* To our amazement *taimaona pasisinaba akabiwa. Wekubvunza panonga pasina iwe.*

We would go on a hunting spree and at times we would be lucky *taiwana dzakahwandiswa or taishaiwa. Tikaiwana yaibva, taitetena kwete zvekutamba, zvekuti* by the time *yekuenda kumba, tinonga taguta. Manje apa sadza rakakumirira rainetsa kudya nekupedza ndopaibuda mushapu zvichinzi idyai mupedze. Hapana akamboti bufu kuti tinombo pfuura nekumabanana.* We had a name for it and *it was not just mabanana chete, asi kuti mapichisi, mangoes nemagwavha. Takazochinja* strategy *taiyenda* late afternoon as soon as the garden workers clocked off for the day *tonotsvaga mabanana edu. Takazoziva kuti* at times *dzimwe ninga dzaiita* disappear *dzaichinjwa ne* the older boys. We never got in trouble over it *kana kukuwara*

.

Part Two.

On our way going home *kuchipisa, taindosambira ku*hospital dam. *Vainge vasingagoni kusambira taienda* to the back of the dam *kumapeto* and swim from there. At the back *kwaiwanda madhaka manje* and the water will be very murky. *Asi taisambira zvakadaro mumadhaka imomo vozogeza ku*front *kwanga kune* clean water before *taenda kumhatso.* The amount of excitement would trigger our decibels too loud; *kuzhakarara nekundofarisa hedu.* We knew *kuti taisabvumidzwa kusambira ikoko asi isu tanga tiine zvivindi.* It brought some happiness within ourselves *kundo* swimmer *ku*dam kwedu. *Ku*main swimming pool *kuchikoro tairambidzwa kuenda ikoko, saka taisakendenga hedu, dam raiwe riri tii. Mamwe mazuva taisvika musina mvura mu*dam.

Tapedza kuswimmer taizora mafuta but there was an agreement *yekuba mafuta kumba kwenyu munhu vese. Mafuta taimaisa mublack polish tin; tose taikwana ipapo. Musi unonga usina kuuya mafuta hapana wai*swimmer. One good afternoon *taenda ku*swimming and we were enjoying ourselves as usual, but the noise levels attracted *Sisi* Emma our house maid. She came to check *kuti* team *iyi ndivanaani vachibva nekumusoro kumugero kwaiiuya nemvura yaipinda mu*dam. *Hapana akawaona, isu taiwe tiri* busy *kufara.*

All of a sudden, the noise seized and there was tranquility which brought everyone's attention *kuti ndiani anyura. Takasimudza musoro mudenga, meso gugaguga naSisi apa vatora hembe dzose*, our demeanour changed. *Vanga vakabata zvimushapu*. I knew what was waiting for me; gap *remambama nemushapu rakabva ratanga. Takabuda mumvura tose; pakarohwa munhu ipapo. Kuzvinzwira pamuviri tsvimbo yembeva. Mishapu yainaya kwete zvekutamba pakabinhwa munhu vose* before *vapihwa hembe dzako uchinanga kumba kwako.*

Inini naVimbai takashapurwa tiri mupushu and frog marched *takananga kugomo tichitinhwa tichikwidza mugero takananga kumba.* All the way home gap *remishapu yainaya vaiziya.* In the evening when dad came home, she reported us. *Pakashapurwa munhu* second round *asi hatina kumira ,bhora mberi, taizoenda ku*swimming on Saturday afternoon but this time noise *taiwe tisingachaiti.*

Some afternoons we would go back and swim *mumugero. Mvura iyoyo ndoyaindodiridziswa ku*garden. We had spots where we used to go and have fun. *Migero yacho* were deep and wide for our size *taikwana imimo* very well. The gravity flow of water would drag us down *mumugero imomo.* The feeling was so good *hakuna akambokuvara mainakidza manje kusambira imomo.* At times we would go to the deeper canal *yaiunza mvura* to the main school garden and the stretches were long. We used to spend long hours *tiriko tichitamba mumvura.*

Once we got to a spot where we could be easily spotted, we would come out, run back for about 800 metres then dive into the canals. This time we were a bit clever, all our clothes would be secured in a 5 kg plastic bag tied on your waste using a belt or string *kuti dzisa tote.* Previous experience *yekushapurwa nekutorerwa hembe yakatimutsa.* At times when we would come for a swim, we would spot the garden workers swimming in the canals. Sometimes we would proceed to go and look for berries near the big dam which was located near the boys' dormitories. The only issue was the berries had deadly peaking thorns but that was never a deterrent to us. These berries were nice red juicy berries, and we would enjoy ourselves *miromo yobva yaita* red.

Other Afternoon activities

We used to enjoy going up the mountains towards Chiremba looking for wild fruits. We had *nzviru, hubva* and *nzambara. Nzambara* are wild berries *dzinoita pane mvura chete*. So, during afternoons *taienda kumba kwasekuru Madanhi* then we grouped up *toenda ku*premier estate looking for *matamba muchin'ando muye neimwe michero. Ku*Premier *taiwana hubva, matohwe asi nzviru dzaivanikwa* towards Mandisodza village kudanga remombe dzaSister Kapenzi. At times we would go all the way to premier estate to collect *ma*oranges but it was a bit of a journey.

The hardest challenge was when we would go *ku*MRID *kumba kwaana* Maxwell *kundodya mahabrois* (Mulberry and blackberry) and swim as well. When it was time to go back we would jog via where Africa University campus is, down via *pavane ma*basketball courts, herding towards Nyangambu river and Mandisodza village. As we got to the hospital *taitanga kusiyana*, Daniel anonga asvika, Moyana boys, then up we go inini and Vimbai. Jogging was the most difficult part as the bigger boys picked speed, *taichema, hapana aikumirira*, tracking behind uchitewera chete. Next mission to go kuMRID you would think twice, *taiwe tawe kuramba kuenda*. We would prefer *kundodya hute kumba kwaana* Nyasha Moyana or near Sekuru Madanhi's place *kwaiwe kune miti yehute.*

Entertainment was not an issue, we would easily entertain ourselves. Next to our house we had a storeroom which was abandoned. After coming back from swimming or banana feasting, we would sneak into the store room via a broken window. The room was peachy black. Once everyone was in *taikurura* our clothes and start singing *kuita morari. Taizhakarara kani tirimo* for a good 2-3 hours *asi zvaitinakidza tapedza topfeka hembe tobuda.* It was very therapeutic for us and up to now I vividly remember it. I was in grade 2-4 there about by then.

One afternoon we drew the attention of Sister Kapenzi and she came to check on us. The problem was that we could not open the door, and she had to reason with us to come out. *Takange tanyarara*, no one was talking. Once we had come out, she wanted to find out *kuti chiii chaimboitika*? Chenjerai had to explain that it was our therapy room where we would come in and sing, nothing else. *Tapedza* we would be calm as ever, each and everyone oenda kumba kwawo, by then the day would be over. After the explanation she just laughed and left us alone. Later, the window was repaired and our *morari* room was no more. Later the *morari* room was taken over by the Chambaras as their kitchen *mevaibikira*.

By Oswald Tariro Darikwa

SECTION THREE (3): HARTZELL HIGH SCHOOL AND TEENAGE LIFE

The National Inter High School Quiz (1992)

In the year 1992, Hartzell High School participated in the National Inter High School Quiz Competition. This competition was usually broadcasted on the Zimbabwe T.V, and a lot of us found it remarkably interesting to watch the competition between famous high schools in Zimbabwe. Schools such as St Georges, Peterhouse College, Churchill, Ellis Robbins etc, were very prominent and dominant on the show, and all these schools were classified as Group A schools or formerly all-white schools. For years we had just enjoyed the show as ordinary TV viewers, until one day at school we were told that our school had been invited to participate.

This was an exciting opportunity to be part of this national show, and as soon as the selection process was started for our school, I was involved. A local competition was organised to be held at the Beit Hall. The competition was held, and the successful participants identified were Rudo Kanjanda, Irvine Chitambo, Walter Mhazo and myself. We were excited to have this opportunity to participate in such a famous t.v show. Mr J.C Sithole, our English teacher, was responsible for the team and getting us ready for the competition. At the time, our school headmaster was Rev J.W Mafondokoto. Hartzell High School itself was not new to national competitions and had indeed famously won two gold medals in the Maths Olympiad competitions, organised at Hartzell by my father, Christopher Mvere. The gold medals were won by Mandirevesa Mugochi and Clement Chinaka, with Kufamina Matsenyengwa and Arthur Mutambara winning silver medals. Hartzell basketball team also was used to winning nationally, led by Mr T. DeWolf.

However, this was the first time for Hartzell to participate in this National Inter High School Quiz. Of course, the idea of being on t.v was appealing to me, over and above competing against other schools over general knowledge questions. The quiz questions ranged from Geography, History, arts entertainment, Science and current news. We set to work the four of us, going through anything we could read that could prepare us for this. From newspapers, encyclopaedias, student's companion, and other specialised reading material we were given.

Our team was set as follows: I was to be the team captain and spokesman, with Rudo and Irvine as the main team, with giant Walter Mhazo as the reserve member. We practiced together and did all we could to be ready, and when the day arrived, we were prayed for in the school assembly. We then set off in Mr J.C Sithole`s Golf car, enroute to Harare where the first round was to be held at Junior School. I remember we stopped at a restaurant for snacks before proceeding to the venue. We were to start at 7pm. We only found out who we were competing against when we got inside the venue.

We were competing against three other schools, and these were St David's Bonda, Watershed High School, and Ellis Robbins. The hall was full, and I remember the famous host, Dr Eric Bloch. We took our seats and I had Rudo to my right and Irvine to my left, and the duel began. I remember the host advising us not to lean into the mic. I was tense but focused. So focused I introduced

Irvine, who was on my left, as sitting to my right! So, I had two right hands that evening.

We were ready for the questions, and right from the start we led the whole pack. I still remember hardly believing that we were leading Ellis Robbins, having seen them on t.v before. I remember one question where we were asked to which country Cape Verde had been a colony to. We could not decide within the first 10 seconds when they sounded that we had 5 seconds left. We could not tell whether it was Portugal or Spain, and in the very last second, I answered, "Portugal!". "Portugal is correct" boomed Mr Bloch and the whole auditorium erupted in cheer.

That moment I felt we had this in our grasp. We had the momentum to capture this win, and so we did. We had given Hartzell its first win in the Inter High School Quiz. It was a great feeling to win like this, and we celebrated on our drive back. It was awesome being announced in the school assembly as having won, a team that was made up of two mission kids.

However, when we went for the second round, it was one round too far ahead for us, and we lost. We had the hardest questions including being asked "who sang Kiss Me Kate in 1953?". Even Walter, who was in the team on that occasion, together with me and Rudo, could not imagine the answer to that, for we were not born then. However, we had the fun of travelling to the big city of Harare to appear on t.v twice, and we looked forward to seeing the episode on tv when it was to be aired.

This story is dedicated to the memory of Walter Mhazo who was the school captain and had such enthusiasm about our participation in the Inter High School Quiz.

By Ndinga Mvere

Mission Boys and Basketball

We loved to call ourselves Mission Boys. There was another group that also claimed that title. These were boys that came to Old Mutare as boarding students and we deemed their claim illegitimate. They were not Mission

Boys. When their guard was down, they would brag about where they were really from. They would paint rosy pictures of the town and cities they hailed from. It was easy as young boys to believe how glorious their places of abode must have been. With the benefit of hindsight, we know now that Old Mutare was the place to be then. We were the real Mission Boys and to this day hold claim to the bragging rights.

Our sport of choice was basketball. It was our 'second religion'. We would play hard and long. The adrenalin rush was what we lived for. Our favourite time on the basketball court was during school vacations. We would meet every day to play, sometimes under moonlight. We did not have the luxury or convenience of lit basketball courts, but we were so grateful to have what we had. At times we would play with worn out basketballs but that was the least of our worries. We would go back home with t-shirts drenched in sweat and would be back on the court again the next day. Occasionally, boys being boys, altercations would flare up but after all had been said and done, the camaraderie that we had transcended our differences. We were the Mission Boys. To this very day we have bonds that were formed on the basketball court that still subsist regardless of geographical distance.

We modelled our style of play after the NBA legends of the day. The competition between our teams was always intense. We pushed ourselves to the limit and loved every moment of it.

The gentleman who introduced us to basketball was Coach Ted DeWolf. His passion for the sport was contagious. Over the years, other coaches would come and go, but for the most part he was there to ensure the love of the game touched as many people as he had interest. He made sure basketballs were accessible, as and when we wanted to play. Looking back, it was a strategy that our school would earn fame for basketball mastery. Our game was head and shoulders above most schools in the country. I remember Nyashanu Secondary School's first boys' basketball team being walloped by an ad-hoc team that had been assembled from an ensemble of random players who were not in the school team. Such was the aptitude for the game at our school.

By Vimbai F D Darikwa

Three Boys Conquer Chiremba

Of the many landmarks at Old Mutare Mission, there's none as colossal as Chiremba mountain. We did not only grow up under its shadow, but it was the subject of much talk and myth. It's well documented that Bishop Hartzell saw his vision for Hartzell and Africa University in this very mountain. There was also a song about Chiremba, "Gomo Guru repa Hatso", that also had connotations to the liberation war. This mountain defined our sunset and so defined when to retreat to our homes after our afternoons or dirt and mud games. In our high school days, Chiremba settled many games at the famous basketball courts during our school holidays, when its shadow encompassed us, thereby starting the beginning of the evening.

Chiremba is a non-rocky mountain and has a low ascend at the bottom, then it gets steep in the middle third, and becomes steeper when you climb to the pinnacle. Our creche, "Rufaro Nursery School" headed by the legendary Mai Mazaiwana, was at the very edges of this mountain, and so were the Grade 1 and Grade 2 blocks, where Gogo Nyakuengama taught for what seemed like an eternity.

So, there we were the Grade 1 class of 83. This class had the likes of my twin brother Tafadzwa, my name mate Farai Mvere, Namatai Mukono, Tadaira Kamangira, Kuda Dhukiso Mukwekwezeke, the then rather vilified Brian (Skata) Chikata, Charles Japondo and Tendai Moyana and myself. On the girl's side were the likes of Chioniso Mudiwa, Zvikomborero Sithole, Rudo Nyandoro and Tsitsi Dzobo. Over the years, cliques formed and dissolved but the clique of my twin brother Tafadzwa, Farai Mvere and myself seemed to last long and was never really dissolved. We even had an understanding that Farai Mvere would be identified as

Fari, while I retained my name Farai, and it has been so to this day.

Since Grade 1, our first real sense of freedom or belief that we had some form of it came after the Form 2 (ZJC) exams. This was the very first time we would be basically free and not having to attend class while the rest of the non-exam classes were in session. It was a time and season not to be missed or let pass by. We spend the afternoons going places, mainly to the ground (soccer field) where we would sit and watch or count cars travelling along the Mutare-Nyanga highway. Back then the timber industry was still big and vibrant in Mutare. So, the sight of the green ERF trucks written "Baringa" and loaded with timber was a marvel, and their exhaust brake noise made the experience even more remarkable. In our circles the Scania, ERF, Leyland debates were also rife because of these sightings.

It was during the Form 2 holidays that Tafadzwa, Fari and I embarked on the unfathomable. We had to make maximum use of the borrowed freedom and we spontaneously decided that we should climb Chiremba. I am not sure how we settled for the idea, but I believe Fari had input into this, because he was always the mischievous ringleader with crazy ideas like smoking leaves, building tree houses and all things naughty. The beginning of the journey was at the B.I (not sure what that stands for to this day) but this is the area where the mission graves are. It was never comfortable passing by the place at night since we grew up hearing a lot about the existence of ghosts at graveyards.

We were glad we were not spotted by some elders or some teacher especially Mr Zvingowanisei, my grade 7 teacher. He was the most feared teacher in all of my primary school years at Old Mutare. Going to high school did not seem to change anything. We still feared him, right into our ZJC years. After this, we navigated the busy area in the lower third where the grass was up to the waist level. The middle part of the climb was the best because there were not many trees and the grass was much lower. During the expedition, we suddenly realised that the fear of the unknown was suppressed by our purpose. I belief the fear of snakes was the highest on the hierarchy of fears because we all personally had experienced some close encounters.

We continued through to the final steep ascend and we sighted the beacon. This is the highest point on the mountain. It marked the success of the mission and, turning around, we looked at the sight of achievement. Looking at Old Mutare mission from that high up is a marvel, we identified our houses, our classroom blocks, the highway, Africa University that had just started, Christmas Pass and other landscapes. We then spent time marvelling and telling stories of things we probably had no idea of. Looking back in time, if it were in this age of technology, we would have flooded our pages with images, emojis and statuses. Since that time, I have never climbed Chiremba again and I am not sure if we could be willing to repeat this adventure again. But as for that afternoon in 1991, three boys conquered Chiremba mountain.

By Farai Nyamajiwa

Lightning Strikes the Gum Tree (1989)

One sunny afternoon, it started raining at Old Mutare Mission. Indeed, there were occasions like this where it could rain whilst a bit of sunshine was peering through the clouds. It was around 4 pm in the afternoon and I was in the lounge at our house. Suddenly, the loudest bang of thunder I had ever heard came through, causing us all to crouch to the floor in shock. It sounded like lightning had struck somewhere close but then again, all our lives we had been used to hearing the thunder and lightning sound, plus seeing its brilliant streaks through the night. On this particular day, we concluded that this was one of the really bad strikes. It had been so loud and scary for many of us.

We did not have to wait for long to understand the impact of the shocking lightning. We started to see the animated exclamations of Villa-bound girls pointing towards something, and we knew something had happened. We ran outside and people were saying *"muGum tree wepa J.C Sithole warohwa nemheni* "(*Gum tree had been struck by lightning*). We began to run towards it and as soon as we got near, we couldn't believe what we were seeing. An almost 60m giant gum tree had been ripped right through its middle, from top to bottom, only leaving a metre above ground undivided. This was a big mature gum tree or Eucalyptus Grandis tree with a diameter of 1.5m. These trees are so tall and are a common feature at Old Mutare. In fact, the drive entrance to Old Mutare is lined with these humongous trees on both sides, with various types of bird's nest in them, including the big white lanky stock birds which fertilise the Marshall section a lot with their droppings. The Eucalyptus Grandis is the most common type of gum tree at Old Mutare, and we peacefully coexisted with these giants. However, seeing one torn like this was an amazing sight to behold for the sheer demonstration of the power of nature, the power of lightning.

It did not take long before the locals, students and teachers included, had gathered around the tree. Deep down everyone was thinking about myths around when lightning strikes. It was believed once lighting strikes it "lays eggs" and returns to strike again in the same place as a way of collecting its eggs. Many myths abound among the Manyika people about how there are two types of lightning. Natural lightning by nature and the unnatural lightning that a wizard can control and use to harm his enemies. However, this one was clearly natural lightning and was more terrifying than anything we could imagine. How could one survive a strike by such a bolt of lightning that had ripped up a whole giant of a gum tree. While people were busy marvelling but staying well clear of the tree in a circle, one of the teachers, Mr T.E DeWolf, popularly known as Ted DeWolf went right up to the tree and he touched the sap coming from the wounded tree as everyone marvelled at his courage to go near whispering, *"Murungu haatyi"* (The white man is fearless).

Years later, the tree dried up and had to be cut down. Once again, that event was spectacular to watch. The whole area around the tree and where it would land was cordoned off. When it came down it was a loud crumble with dry branches flying everywhere and dust engulfing everyone. That was the end of that gum tree, except for its stump which was left to continue. When I passed through Old Mutare in 2019, even the gum tree stump had been removed. It was disappointing that such a special tree stump with rich history was removed.

Where were you on that day and when was it?

Mazvita Nzara: 1992: If I remember well, we were writing exams. The sound was so loud.

Washy Musesengwa: It was 1989, I was in Form 3. Julie Mutenda fainted.

Tariro Darikwa: Pakaipa kufenda ne mheni. The bang was so loud we heard it from the hospital side zvikanzi pane chikuru cheya rowa.

Namatai Mukono: I think it was 1989

Rudo Chifamba: I think 1989. We were in class (form 1C) and Ophius Chishawa hid under a desk.

By Ndinga Mvere

My Encounter with the Mysterious

Old Mutare Mission is inextricably etched somewhere in my heart. It is here that I was born and bred. My worldview is to a great extent influenced and informed by my experiences at the mission. It was here that I first fell in love with a girl, but never summoned enough courage to tell her how I felt about her. I know this gets you excited, but that's me getting ahead of myself. I'll get back to this juicy story at the end of my narrative. Mutare

Mudhara is another appellation that we loved to give this place that gave me abode for over a quarter of a century. Literally! For my dear departed mother, it was more. She was a nurse at O.M.M hospital for a whopping 47 years. She started working at O.M.M right out of nursing school before she was married to my dad. While others checked out at 60, my mother worked past her retirement. The skills flight that hit the country at the time made it possible for older nurses to continue working past the official retirement age. That preface to my story I hope gives me bragging rights for the title of whatever that it entitles me to.

O.M.M is where I was introduced to Christianity. It could not have been any other way since the centre was established as a place, among other things, for worship. Church attendance in our family was mandatory. It was an unwritten rule. My father was a devout Christian who modelled the love for the Holy Scriptures for me. Having said that, some things as I was growing up did not make sense, but now with the benefit of hindsight and experience, connecting the dots is a lot easier. However, some things will forever remain a mystery like the story I am about to share with you. It is a fascinating, if not mystical incident that happened when I was doing my 'A' level studies. One afternoon as I was walking to school, everything out of my left eye became blurry. I could not fathom what was going on. When I checked in the mirror later that day, my worst fears were confirmed. A cataract had developed and was clouding my vision. My mother, as noted, was a nurse but I remember going to my dad for help instead. He gave scrutiny to my eye and confirmed that indeed there was a visible cataract.

The following day, my dad instructed me to go and present a live chicken to a certain elderly man that lived at the periphery of O.M.M. I met the gentleman close to his house. All he wanted to know was my totem after I had told him the purpose of my visit. I bade him goodbye and went back home. The following day, as dramatically as the cataract had appeared, it was gone. My eye could see clearly just like nothing ever transpired. Just like that! It was amazing. This gentleman neither touched me, nor said a prayer of sorts over me. The chicken I gave him was an ordinary broiler we raised at home for sale and for our consumption. What had just happened?

When I confronted my dad about the issue, his response left me with more questions than answers. "There are people in this world that know things that we are oblivious to." That was his brief and dismissive answer. To this day, the cataract has never come back – not that I would want it to. I never had the opportunity to establish what really happened. Sadly, both my dad and the gentleman are late, and I have no one to answer the barrage of questions I have. I waited too long. This trait admittedly and regrettably led me to lose my first love, again I waited too long.

She was beautiful. Her smile dismantled all the high school tough guy infrastructure that I was known for. We became good friends. We would walk to and from school together. She made going to school all the more enjoyable. Teenage relationships were not particularly encouraged at O.M.M. Parents would rather see us concentrating on our academic pursuits. Her name will remain anonymous for the obvious reasons. She pulled all the right strings in my heart. The mere thought of that epoch in my life as I was growing up at O.M.M brings back in a sneaky enjoyment in my heart. I remember telling myself that one day I would tell her how she made my world go round, and how I wanted her to be my girl. I waited too long.

By Vimbai Darikwa

SECTION FOUR (4): MISSION LIFE AND CULTURE

Weddings at Old Mutare Mission

Weddings were always a big deal at Old Mutare Mission (OMM). The mission was usually the one-stop-shop for the ceremony, celebratory lunch, and reception. The only thing that sometimes got "outsourced" to other venues was the bridal party and family photo shoot; which would happen at more picturesque venues like the botanical gardens at Larochelle, or the ones in Mutare city centre.

Weddings were community affairs, and preparations would start many months ahead of the big day. One key feature of weddings at the mission (and I suppose anywhere else in the "80"s and "90"s Zimbabwe) was that everyone was invited, whether they got any actual wedding invite or not. Formal invites would go out to everyone, but this was only a formality. Even if someone was unintentionally not invited, they could certainly show up on the day and be welcomed with open arms - participation by the entire community was implicitly expected and accepted.

The Ceremony

The big day would start in our grand and beloved Ehnes Memorial Church. Very early in the morning (or night before), women in the community would decorate the church with flowers, glittery ribbons and other festive accessories. The bride would be dressed in one of the inner chambers of the church by a well-appointed group of "*vana mai vepamission*". Since the bride or groom was almost always a 'mission kid" or a mission resident, the bridesmaids and groomsmen would get ready at the family home.

From about 9am onwards, all roads led to the majestic Ehnes Memorial and the ceremony would commence around 10am. There would be so much excitement about seeing how beautiful the bride's dress was, how beautiful the bridesmaids were bedecked, and of course, how many "steps" (tiers) the cake was. For some reason, the groom's outfit was not ever quite an object of anticipation or conversation.

The script for the ceremony was pretty standard: the community filed into the church, and once the church was reasonably full and all family was present, the bridal party would file in and take their seats right at the front. The reverend, usually one of the reverends at O.M.M, would preach a shortish sermon then lead the couple in taking their vows. After signing of the marriage documents, the cake cutting would happen. The much anticipated (and usually chaotic) distribution of the cake would follow. The expectation was that everyone would take one small piece of the cake, however reality was stalky different. Some would hilariously grab fistfuls of cake, resulting in there not being enough cake to go around. Those sitting at the back of the church usually were the casualties of cake shortages, so there was an unwritten rule to try and sit as close to the front as possible in order to not miss out on the delicacy, that was the wedding cake.

Then there would be the "umbowo" section were family and friends would give short testimonials of the bride or groom, share advice on how to successfully navigate married life and how to live happily ever after. Prayer would mark the end of the ceremony and the guests would file out of the church; waiting outside to shower confetti on the bridal party as they walked out of the church.

The Wedding Lunch

Next stop would be the Junior Boys Dining Hall. If cake eating part was a favourite for most guests, the lunch was probably the best part at all weddings. The entire guest and bridal party would make their way to the dining hall. The wedding party and a few 'VIPs" had the privileged position of being ferried by car on the half a kilometre trek from the church. The rest would walk and queue up for lunch.

Cooking for wedding lunches was another element that mission folks had got down to an art. Everyone helped. Cooking was crowdsourced - different households would opt in to prepare certain dishes and bring those to the dining hall on the day of the wedding. The dining hall kitchen would be the central hub of activity. Without fail, a beast would be slaughtered and there would be large cast iron pots full of aromatic beef stew bubbling away. No wedding would be complete without '*mabhodha esadza*' which community folks would happily dive in to cook. By about 1pm, the hall would be open for business; ready to dish out typical wedding fare of rice *ne*chicken with coleslaw salad as well as *sadza nenyama* (beef) and veggies. The former was usually served to the "High Table" which comprised wedding party as well as close family and friends. The latter would largely be served to the broader community. Some folks fell somewhere in between and would get various combinations of rice, chicken, sadza *or nyama*. .Nyama yainaka iyoyo.This hierarchical pecking order was largely accepted - folks would happily tuck into lunch, wash the food down with a bottle of soda and head to the Beit Hall for the final event on the itinerary - the reception.

The Reception

This final act is where the whole community "let their hair down". Preparations for the receptions would start months in advance; with the bridal party "*vachidzidzira masteps*" which meant practicing dances or dance moves. This would be traditional dances like the waltz, foxtrot, and the like, but eventually there were home-grown variations and outright inventions - all were embraced and loved.

Then there was the disco and the D-jay! As with anything, some discos and D-jay were better than others. Needless to say, being able to secure and top tier disco and D-jay was the mark of an exceptional wedding. By the time the guests finished lunch and started to file towards the iconic Beit Hall, the disco would be all set up and festive music could be heard blaring from the massive loudspeakers.

At some point between lunch and the reception, the wedding party and their "VIP'S" would break away for their photo shoot. Usually this involved driving to town or Larochelle, so there would be a 'black-out" period where the bridal party would be AWOL, so to speak. The disco and D-jay filled that vacuum. The crowd would enjoy whatever was hot on the music scene at that given time. Some favourites that quickly come to mind are Leonard Dembo's *"Chitekete"* and "*Sharai*", Brenda Fassie's "Weekend Special" as well as countless reggae and r 'n' b hits.

An hour or so into the disco the bridal party would make their grand entrance and do several "steps". Then would come the "zvipo' section. This was when family, friends and the community would give their gifts to the bride and groom. Each gift was recorded and announced. There was a lot of pomp and fanfare around giving and announcement of gifts. The bigger the gift, the bigger were the associated theatrics. Gifts varied from large monetary ones (usually from parents and siblings of the bride and groom) to smaller amounts from distant acquaintances and everything in between. Gifts also took the form of household items - stoves and fridges (usually from parents and close family), pots and pans, cutlery and other trinkets. Every gift, large or small, was acknowledged and appreciated.

At this point, the format of the festivities would weave from bridal party dances to gift announcements to guests taking to the dance floor. This freestyle format usually signalled the conclusion of the festivities. People would slowly start to leave for their respective homes. It was always the end of a happy day with utterances like: "ii muchato wanakidza uyu", "muchatiswa anga akachena", "kuzoti hembe dzevaperekedzi kunaka", "disco ranga richinakidza anhuwe.", "keke racho mariona here? 4 steps! Zvitsva kani - tajaira 3 steps". Along with the positive comments would be the odd "Keke harina kusvika kwatanga takagara…" or "tashaya makokokora (Coca Cola)" or "nyama yapera maUsher aakutosvika patable patangatiri…" The positive always outweighed the negative and the wedding would be the talk of the mission for weeks to come or until the next wedding; when our beloved Old Mutare Mission family would once again host and support another set of happy and successful nuptials.

By Rudo Kanjanda Chifamba

The Sanctuary

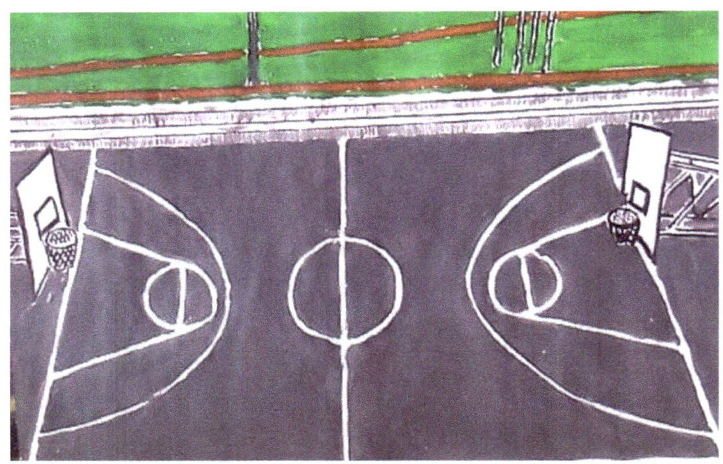

Having grown up and spent most of my life at Old Mutare Mission, there are so many places within the mission that I hold dear to my heart, but one place that really takes the crown for me is the basketball court. Quite the opposite to what most people would like to believe, it is not even the big tournaments that were held during the school days that come to my mind first, but the role the courts played during the holidays in entertaining and shaping the lives of many 'mission boys'. In fact, the place was more of a retreat than anything else. Like wild animals making their way to a watering hole, most 'mission boys' from the various sections, would converge at the basketball courts towards sunset. This included not only the basketball players, but also those who would just come to watch, and chat the noon away. Mostly, these were people who were way older than I was, but because they were friends with my older brother, Kuda, it was quite easy for them to embrace us like their very own young brothers, and this afforded us the opportunity to receive a form of socialization that I still treasure, even up to now.

One of the things I learned quickly just by going to the basketball courts was that I could do anything, if only I put the necessary work into it. In other words, I learned to dream at an early age. I still remember seeing the likes of Simba 'Simbz' Mvere and Tonderai 'Kunde' Nyamombe, who were not even as tall as most people would expect basketball players to be, but were very fierce competitors on the court. Being a guy who was not tall as well, but who really enjoyed the game, I always drew inspiration from watching these guys play. I still recall making a resolution to be as good as them, and hopefully, be able to receive the honor of being selected to play with these guys someday. In a bid to improve, my age mates and I would go collect the ball as early as

2pm either from the Mvere or Nyamajiwa residence, who were all so kind enough to give it to us. We would play all noon until somewhere like 4pm, when we would vacate the court for the terraces in order for the 'big boys' to play. We did this religiously, with a lot of hope tied up in our hearts, that someday, we would be playing in the senior league. So, we also learned not only how to dream, but how to hope as well, and holding on to that hope tenaciously.

At one time, there were two half-court teams, namely Chicago Bulls, led by Simba 'Simbz' Mvere, and Orlando Magic, led by the likes of Gwinyai 'Gwinz' Nyamajiwa. How they picked the names, I do not know, but I guess those were some of the best sides in the NBA then. They competed fiercely to the extent that one could feel the tension, even from the terraces. It was almost as if there was some prize money at the end of the series of games. Fouls were heavily disputed, bringing most games to a halt each time that happened. But what I liked the most was that, after all this, there was no bad blood between the players, and that is when I began understanding the spirit of friendly competition. I understood that it is normal for people to compete against each other, and if kept healthy, competition can challenge people to achieve things they never thought they could.

It certainly is unfair to try and use words to describe how the basketball courts were a haven for us. They forged some sort of brotherhood and mutual respect amongst the 'mission boys', which I would like to believe still exists up to now. This was not just amongst the players, but everyone who came there, even to spectate. I still remember the likes of Namatai Mukono, Farai Mvere, and the late Stewart Ndadzungira, amongst others, who were not even basketball players, but whose presence on the terraces was equally important as that of the players. It was usually this audience that would effortlessly light up the terraces with laughter. And when the series of games would end, the players would come join in the conversations, whilst catching their breath. It is during moments like these that things like the famous New Year's party would be organized, and although some of us were still a bit too young to attend, I really liked how it fostered that much needed unity.

It is quite easy for a stranger or a passerby to quickly dismiss the basketball courts as mere paved surfaces with hoops, but for us, they meant more than that, and still do. The relationships and valuable life lessons that I still hold dear in my heart, are a simple reflection of how the basketball courts were more of a sanctuary than anything else.

By Tapiwa Sithole

Rangariro

Ndakazvarirwa pamission tikakurirapo . Ndakatanga kudzidza ku Creche tichidzidziswa namai Mutimbanyoka na Mai Mazaiwana kuma 1970s. Grade 1 ndakadzidziswa na Mai Nyakuengama wari mai Mufundisi zvakare sezvo murume wawo aiwa Station Chairman Rev Nyakuengama. Headmaster Principal aiwa Baba Dangarembga , Boarding Master Baba Marima , Director ari MBaba Maenzanisa, Matron Mai Zisengwe, Mission farm kwaiwa na Broumquest. Primary school headmaster aiwa Baba Nyanhanda. Matron aiwa Mai Kapenzi.

Painakidza uye paityisa zvekuti waisango fambafamba usina kwekuenda. Taienda ku tuckshop ko sangana newamwe pama school holidays . Chingwa chaisiyiwa makuseni seni ne dairiboard pa Tuckshop. Kana pasina chingwa taienda kwa Friiks

Baba Chaita aidriver tractor . Paiwe zvakare ne Printing press ye United Methodist. Vafundisi vakateedzana waivepo , Muzorewa ,Nyakuengama, Chikafu, Mubiro , Nhiwatiwa , Marange , Chingonzo.

Baba Dewolf an Baba Degrant ndiwo wakagadzira maring e Basketball rings. Form 3 Block yakawakwa nana Baba Saungweme nana Baba Assam.

Garden echikoro aiwe panzira yekuenda kuhospital maiwe nema Orange. Baba Dewolf wakatanga Garden raiwe petyo ne Kraal.

Painakidza , Paityisa . Taipinda UMYF ku BI pamaholidays. Danga remombe re Hospital raiwa taakuenda kupremier, mombe dze Nherera. Re Boys boarding raiwa papaine maintenance. Villa yaiwe nemombe dzayo waakuenda kwa Friiks. Kwakuine rimwe danga kumission Farm . Papaine maorchard .

Discipline yanga yakawandisa . Zvaita sekuti taiwe in a shell tisingaziwi outside world. Taipedza maholiday tiri pamission.

Pamaholiday taitamba basketball tapihwa mabhora acho na Mr Dewolf. Ndakazombo tsikinywa pahuro ndichibatsira kuwaka umba ya Mr Dewolf kupurazi kwawo tiri pamwe na Chenjerai Chambara naMoses Dozva. Africa University yakawakwa takatarisa tikadaidzwa wo ko batsira .

By Ndozvi Kamangira

SECTION FIVE (5): TRIBUTES

A Childhood Buddy Reminisces:

Tribute To the Late Mr Albert Chenai Darikwa

My earliest recollections of Chenai stretch back to our infantile days at Old Mutare Mission in the 1960s. The

mission place was our cradle of genesis and we shared common pedigree from then. Since so many people know and will write so much about this special friend of mine, I shall focus on our first 10 years of existence on this planet.

The Methodist mission was a mosaic of lifestyles and living standards, but our homes were in the humble section called 'Marshall Village' where throngs of kids roamed Marshall roads. Dust was part of our lives; as a result, we all looked the same. Allow me to recall a few of Chenai's dust mates; Goodloe Zisengwe, Lincoln Haparimwi, Sekai Ndemera, Tendai Mawoyo and Ngoni Maenzanise. We ran around, played, rolled, climbed hills, fell into gullies, swam, dived in rivers and puddles of mud, screamed and fought anything that disturbed our peace as a team. Armed with our sticks and stones, we were a menace to dogs, cats, snakes and chameleons that dared cross our dusty paths.

On one particular day, Chenai and I broke our gang rules and ventured out on our own to a bushy area beyond the sports fields. An unusual hissing sound drew our attention to a whole brigade of "*masvosve mukange*" on a full marching parade. I cannot quite think of the English word for these venomous black ants, I suppose you can fill this in. These ants are best left alone but I do not know what entered our juvenile minds to attack and trample the whole army with our sandaled feet! The little soldiers were quick to crawl all over us delivering the most excruciating stings we ever endured. Our desperate screams of agony drew help from Teacher Makoni who "airlifted" us one in each of his strong arms to safety. Appropriate reprimand was delivered to glorious jeers from our fellow gangsters. To this very day the sight of black ants strike fear in my heart.

Our toys were simple; old motor tyres, old bicycle rims, *ndege dzemazhonje* (toy planes), *ndande* (catapults, which doubled as self defence ammunition, particularly against ferocious dogs). Chenai was particularly blessed to have a tricycle which was quite a solid contraption for it could courier the whole gang with ease. Our sporting profile was even more elementary, soccer using a home-made plastic ball, 'block myself games' which was essentially hide and seek and *chivhiriri mukange*.

Before I go to our academic life, allow me to relate the last and most dangerous stunts Chenai and gang were involved in. This was the tractor game. The mission maintenance department was privileged to have an old Messy Ferguson tractor and trailer which was an irresistible attraction to the gang. This particular game was strictly the preserve of seasoned guys like Chenai and I. The young new arrivals like Brian were not permitted. Each time Baba Chaita the driver was about to start off, we would sneak up to the back end of the trailer and hang on with our hands, with our feet freely dangling down. Oblivious of the bunch of unwanted passengers, the poor driver would start off, slowly picking up speed while the onlookers jeered in admiration of the little heroes. The special trick was to decide on the critical point to jump off before the little tractor reached dangerous speed. On this particular day, after all of us had lept off, our hero took a bit too long to let go and jump. The roadside cheering party was wild, and the hero jumped off! I recall a whole cloud of dust going up, in panic we dashed to the scene were a hilarious spectacle awaited us. While his face was unrecognizable, the upper lip was grossly protuberant. As was our culture during such events, we enthusiastically helped him up and cautiously escorted him and presented him to his mother! The rest of the gang then vanished immediately.

Allow me to finish with a brief description of our educational roots. Rufaro Nursery School was patched on the foothills of Chiremba mountain. This was the very first educational institute Chenai attended. I recall the whole bunch of kids singing "*tumawoko tumawoko tunoita zvakanaka....*" and so many other rhymes under the watchful eye of Sissy Angie Marima *naMai* Mutimbanyoka. The warm fresh buns were perhaps our greatest motivation to attend crèche, more so even during the bitterly cold winters.

The very old part of our local mission primary school was called the "kraal school". The buildings were old but we were excited to start school in 1971, and worked our way to grade 4 in 1974. Mrs Munjoma was our grade 1 mistress, Teacher Makoni, grade 2, Mai Nzara, and Mai Chitsenga between maternity leaves, took us for grade 3. The revered Mr Sithole "Chigadzira-memba" was our grade 4 master. Chenai was naturally left-handed, which then was unfortunately an inadmissible misalignment of a handwriting skill by educators of those years. No amount of reprimand could change his dexterity but his hand writing was exceptionally smart.

I deliberately choose to stop at 1974. Yes, I could go on and on relating the life I shared with my friend, but out of all this, I appreciated the gift of a caring friend. He was a humorous companion, intelligent, analytical and compassionate.

May Chenai's spirit rest in the arms of our Lord Jesus.

By Dr Ralph Nhiwatiwa

Tribute to Shaire T. Nhiwatiwa

I have tried to scratch the back of my mind to my earliest memories with Shaire, and I keep seeing us when we were around four to five years racing each other with old car tyres as a group, with the likes of Jonah Dozva, Fungai and Kufamina Matsenyengwa, Tendai Chikata, and Daniel Chiwandika, along the Marshall 2 dust road between our houses, and Shaire would win most of those races. Those races were kind of our own 'Fast and Furious" back then with everyone pushing their old tyre making vehicle sounds such as "vhuuumm" and even the gear changing sounds "GuchuGrrrrk ka"

I also remember when he got his bicycle, that must have been around 1980/81, which had been passed down from his older brothers, we passionately called it 'Chiramba Kusakara'. That is the first bicycle I ever rode in my life, and that is when I also learnt to ride. Back then, bicycles for kids were few and our fathers' bicycles were a no-go area, and certainly not for a child to learn to ride from. So, most of the bunch of us, from Marshall 2, we learnt to ride through Shaire's bicycle, which we would all line up to take turns to ride in the football pitch at the end of Marshall 2. Shaire was very patient with all of us as we took turns to learn to ride on his bicycle, and falling off it; you know how it is when you are learning to ride. In those early days, we also used to make toy wire cars, and designing the cars was a big deal, especially for the less artistic minded ones like some of us. Shaire was always readily available to give a hand or give a design of one of his old cars, even sharing the small wires we used to attach the frames, what we called "Zvipombo".

As we grew older through primary school, Shaire's academic excellence and prowess on the 100 meters was clearly remarkable and outstanding. I remember in 1984/85, he qualified for the Manicaland Primary Schools Athletics provincial team, that travelled to Masvingo for the national competitions, where he won a medal, which was presented to him during the weekly assembly at H.C.P.S. Shaire was hardworking and dedicated in what he did, and despite being naturally talented, he still practiced hard to fine tune his skill. In preparation for his athletics competitions, I used to train with Shaire every morning at 6 am. We would run from Marshall 2 to Lamour bottle store and back (about 5 to 6km) in about 45 minutes to an hour.

Even though Shaire did not do his studies at Hartzell High, he kept in touch with all of us, his peers, during holidays where we would study together and play our famous social basketball in the evenings at the basketball courts. Shaire was also an interestingly fun character who enjoyed playing pranks. I remember some time in 1991, he made a stink bomb and released it in the Beit Hall during the Saturday afternoon function. He must have underestimated the strength of the stink bomb because it drove everyone out of the Beit Hall, and some of the students were not amused by the prank. I remember he quickly apologized, and the Saturday afternoon mood returned to normal, after the smell of the stink bomb had gone down.

Shaire grew up to form and own a successful advertising company in Harare, from 1996 to 2002, called "Dream Coats", named after the biblical story of Joseph's coat/tunic of many colours (Genesis 37 verse 3). The company did adverts/campaigns for large corporations such as Netone, Econet, Innscor (Bakers Inn) and it also printed T-shirts, post cards and car bumper stickers with humorous Christian messages such as, "Repent there is no fire brigade in hell" or "Why rush, Jesus travelled by donkey". Shaire was always a committed Christian who believed in our Lord Jesus Christ and sought his guidance in everything he did.

Shaire maintained a simple low-profile lifestyle, and the book he read the most, was the Holy Bible, seeking deeper understanding of the good word always. He was such a deeply committed believer in the inside than what he showed outwardly. Shaire was like a book with a cover that could easily mislead about the contents inside the book, and it would only take one to read the book to fully understand its contents. He always used to say, "If you meet someone who knows, then there is no problem, or if you meet someone who doesn't know, then there is still no problem, but if you meet someone who thinks he knows, then you have a huge problem!"

I believe one way or the other, Shaire touched our lives in many ways than we can all explain, especially those of us who knew and interacted with him. I cherish all the times I spent with him, and up to now I still reflect on some conversations we used to have, as I still find them very relevant up to now. His presence will always be deeply missed.

May His Soul Rest in Eternal Peace.

By Tapuwa W L Nzara

APPENDIX

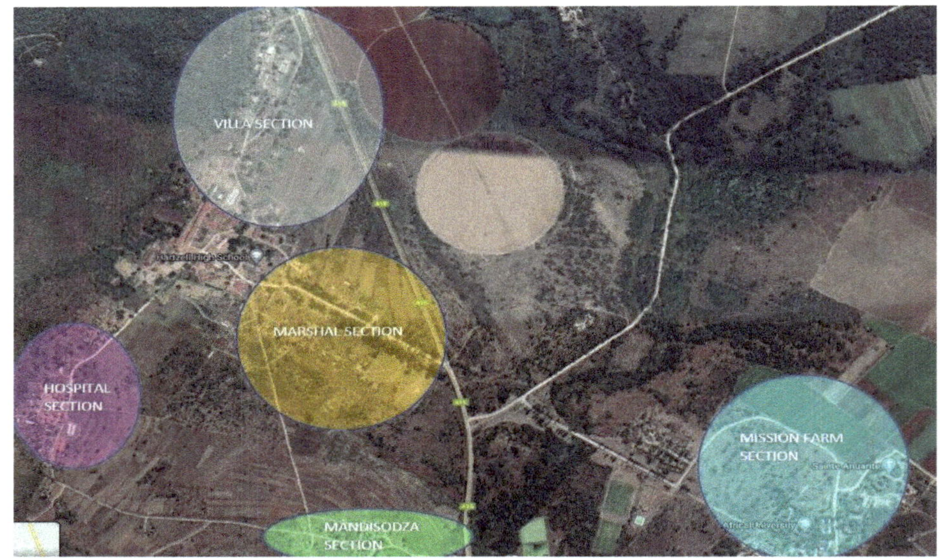

OLD MUTARE MISSION SECTIONS

Old Mutare Mission Sections

1 Marshal Section

2 Hospital Section

3 Villa Section

4 Mandisodza Section

5 MRID

Marshall Section 1980s/90s

Residents of Marshall Section 80S/90s

1	Rusere	22	L Matsenyengwa	38	Chambara
2	Makaruse	23	Makaruse	39	Katsidzira
3	S Sithole	24	Mlambo	40	Haas/Schweda
4	Muringapi	25	Mushonga	41	Matanga
5	Dozva	26	T Bepe	42	Jambaya
6	Maintenance Dept	27	Pfukwa	43	Mashiri
7	Dzimati	28	Segura	44	Dangarembga
8	Katsidzira	29	Musindo	44	Rugayo
9	Ndadzungira	30	Thobani	44	Mukwekwezeke
10	Manjiche	31	Mutimbanyoka	44	Mafondokoto
11	Chivandika	32	Mashiri	44	Mutasa
12	Chidziya	33	Marezu	45	Jumburus
13	Dozva	34	Masvikeni	46	Church Hall
14	Maringapasi	35	Nyanhanda	47	Ehnes Memorial Church
15	Chikata	36	Stn Chairman	48	Tuck Shop /Central Offic
16	Makoni	36	Rev Chikafu	49	New building
17	Jambaya	36	Rev Mumbiro	50	Football Pitches
18	Nzara	36	Rev Nhiwatiwa		
19	Nyanhanda	36	Rev Marange		
20	Nhiwatiwa	36	Rev Chingonzo		
21	C Matsenyengwa	37	New building		

134

HOSPITAL SECTION 1980s/90s

Residents of Hospital Section 80s/90s

51	Dozva		56	Waiting Mothers
52	Kapenzi	57		66
	Kurewa	58		67

VILLA SECTION 1 1980s/90s

Figure 1 Villa Section Map 1980s

Residents of Villa Section 80s/90s

71 Tuckshop
72 Whitehouse
73 Beit Hall
74 DeWolf
75 JC Sithole
86 F Sithole
87 Dr Teepe
87 Ms Strickland
87 Ms Bronick
88 Ms Tarumbwa

76 Nyamajiwa
77 Pastor Kupa
78 Mhere
78 Nhiwatiwa
78 Reevis
78 Ngirandi
78 Makande
78 Madondo
79 Muguma
80 Nyakuengama
81 Gumbere
82 Mvere
83 Mukono
84 Chidawanyika
85 Mukwekezeke
Musesengwa
89 Kraal (Grade 1-3)
90 Kreche
91 Borehole
*45 See Marshall Section Lis

VILLA SECTION 2 1980s/90s

Residents of Villa Section2 80s/90s

120 Shamu
121 Matongo
122 Mutimamba
123 Mawoko
124 Mudiwa
125 Ms Taylor
Whitfields
126 Mazaiwana
127 Zisengwe
Mataranyika
128 Maenzanise
129 Kaindiyese
130 Chieza
131 Rufaro Girls Hostel Alev
132 Villa Girls Boarding

MANDISODZA SECTION 1980s/90s

Residents of Mandisodza Section 80s/90s

92	Mission Store	101	Mudiwa
93	Butchery (BJ Mutasa)	102	Muguma
94	Mukotsanjera Garage	103	Nyazika Mbuya
95	Julius Bepe	104	Sekuru Taibo
96	Noisi	105	Saungweme
97	Makamanzi	106	Rev Moyo
98	Maenzanise	107	Chakadonha
99	Mandisodza Hall	108	Nyamombe
100	Japondo	109	Bhebhe

www.ingramcontent.com/pod-product-compliance
Lightning Source LLC
Chambersburg PA
CBHW040537170726
48295CB00012B/498

9781835383933